No Ordinary Life

By

Peter Stokes

Published in 2013 by FeedARead Publishing

A CIP catalogue record for this title is available from the British Library.

No Ordinary Life

The previously untold personal story of a young Commando and SAS soldier in World War 2, from Sark to Stalag VIIA. On his death, Sergeant H Stokes of 2nd SAS left a journal that revealed what his life had been like growing up in the shadow of approaching war, and then describing his part in operations behind enemy lines in France, the Mediterranean and Italy. In August 1939, an 18 year old Stokey, as he was known to his war-time comrades, left his home in Birmingham to attend a two-week Territorial Army (TA) Camp in Devon, and in those two-weeks he was mobilised when Hitler invaded Poland. This young TA soldier would never put on civilian clothes for another six years. This book charts his journey through 12 Commando, his move to the Small Scale Raiding Force (SSRF) and eventually on to the 2nd Special Air Service (SAS), and his capture, escape, and recapture behind enemy lines in Italy and Germany in 1944.

This book could not have been written without the help of my family and friends who encouraged me to bring the story to print. A very special thank you must go to two people, Chip (you know who you are) and Dr Tom Keene. Tom's outstanding work on the formation of the Small Scale Raiding Force, published in the book 'Hand of Steel', allowed me to confirm and add some small detail to my work. My father wanted this published for his grand children and their children. We will remember him.

For Ben, Sophie and Joelle. You didn't know him but may you, through this book, be closer to your Grandfather.

Contents

Foreword

List of Illustrations and maps

A. Ambleteuse

B. MTB 344

C. Stokey 1939

D. Anderson Manor

E. SSRF Dory Drills

F. Sark landing area

G. Lampedusa

H. Map of Pantellria, Lampedusa and Sicliy

I. HMS Unshaken

J. Sgt H Stokes 2nd SAS 1944

K.   Horace and Joan Stokes

L. Father and Son RAF College Cranwell 1984

Sgt H Stokes 2nd SAS

To Stokey:

We are the Pilgrims, master; we shall go,

Always a little further: it may be

Beyond the last blue mountain barred with snow,

Across that angry or that glimmering sea.

(The Golden Journey to Samarkand)

FOREWORD

The Second World War (WW2) started in September 1939 and ended in August 1945. Over this period millions of soldiers, sailors, airmen and civilians died. Whilst it is now a distant memory, many people alive today will know something about this war, either through studying it in history, through buying a poppy or, if they were very privileged, through listening to the stories of their relatives who experienced the horror and atrocities of 'total' war at first hand.

There have been countless books written about WW2 and the subject has been covered from many different perspectives. Some recall history in technical terms such as the types and performance of aircraft or tanks, some analyse the factual tactical accounts of great battles. Others record events as they unfolded, captured through the records of generals, Presidents and war correspondents.

A number of quite special books recount the story from a very personal perspective, through the eyes of the soldiers, sailors and airmen who were committed to battle. Every soldier's personal experience of WW2 would be different. For many, the War would be characterised by being conscripted into the armed services, undertaking basic training, followed by waiting and then being launched into battle which for most young soldiers would have been terrifying and confusing. Despite this, some soldiers made it through the war without ever having to take a life but this made them no less brave.

A very small number of men saw active service behind enemy lines, where they were often required to kill the enemy in hand to hand fighting and close combat. These were the men of the Commandos, Airborne Forces, Special Boat Service and Special Air Service. This book tells the very personal story of an ordinary, modest young man whose extraordinary exploits were captured in his personal journal that came to light when he died on 26th December 1986. Quite remarkably, many of the things he revealed in the weeks before his death had never before been shared with anyone. For a number of reasons, however, it has taken nearly 25 years to bring his story to print.

No Ordinary Life is therefore a tribute to a man, my father, with whom I had the great pleasure and honour to share his closest secrets in the days before he died. Despite his detailed recollection of many things, the book has required additional research and I am grateful to a number of other sources, such as Dr Tom Keene, that have allowed me to fill in some small gaps.

I have also drawn on my own experience as an officer with long service in the Royal Air Force Regiment, working closely with the British Army and Royal Marines on operations and during training. The words in the first and last chapters are mine and mine alone. At the beginning I have tried to add a short introduction to help readers who may have no understanding of how the armed forces operate. I briefly explain the size and organisational structure of units; the strategic context; the planning required to deploy and lead troops on operations; and simple things such the grit and determination required to overcome one's personal fear and apprehension when stepping into the unknown.

My attempts to explain some of these things in very basic terms may offend some ex-servicemen, and some of those who are still serving, but I hope people can see beyond the simple explanations and focus on the purpose of this book, which is not to tell the story of a unit, but to recount the wartime journey of a young man who, like so many others, had to risk his life time and again.

Horace Leonard Stokes, known to his friends and comrades as 'Stokey', originally wanted to write about his life because he had a feeling of living through something that had been quite remarkable and unbelievable, and he wanted to capture this for his children and their children.

Before his death, however, he reflected that every generation, as it grows older, also sees dramatic changes, such as the loss of an Empire or the Moon landings. He therefore felt that the things that had happened to him and thousands of people like him, were not in fact truly remarkable - it just felt like it at the time.

I disagree. Whilst the stories of our very brave Servicemen and women fighting in recent conflicts (the Falklands, Iraq and Afghanistan) are fresh in our minds, there is also a need to reflect on the things that happened in a war where the horror and scale stretch beyond the realms of most people's comprehension. Despite this, many ex-servicemen and women will recognise the memories, lessons and reflections of large scale war and the sacrifices made by ordinary men and women, called upon to place themselves in perilous danger.

Additionally, there is something new in the telling of true war stories capturing the experiences of those who serve. Soldiers, even those serving with the Special Forces, are now more able to reveal the detail of their operations in a way that my father would not have been able to comprehend. He was of a generation that believed the strength of the SAS, and what it did, should remain secret. Indeed, I fully remember his reaction to the pictures that launched the SAS into the public eye on 5th May 1980 when their bravery, skill and aggression was captured on live TV during the Iranian Embassy Siege in London.

His reaction to this was to put away his Regimental tie and blazer (that he would wear on special occasions with quiet pride and anonymity) and they would never again see the light of day. Therefore, this story could never have been published whilst my father was alive. Additionally, he wanted to forget about his war exploits as he felt incredibly guilty for having survived whilst so many of his best mates perished. He never spoke of it to friends, family, or ex-members of the SAS. Not once did he attend a reunion.

There are other reasons why it's has taken me over 25 years to get this story into print. It could never have been written whilst my mother was alive; she loved my father very much and being part of this would have been too painful for her. She lived with a man who never shared his inner secrets about the war but she knew he paid a price in life for being one of the few who survived.

Lastly, my own life was occupied with frequent lengthy military tours of duty and long spells of arduous training. Therefore, having retired from Armed Forces a few years ago I felt that I had some spare time to do justice to my father's story. So this book is based on the exploits and personal account of my father's life as a Commando and SAS soldier in WW2. Someone who left his home in Birmingham, as a teenager, in August 1939, to attend a two-week Territorial Army (TA) Camp, and during those two-weeks was mobilised when Hitler invaded Poland.

That young TA soldier would not put on civilian clothes again for another six years. It charts his journey through 12 Commando, his move to the Small Scale Raiding Force (SSRF) and eventually on to the 2nd Special Air Service (SAS), and his capture, escape, and recapture behind enemy lines in Italy and Germany in 1944. It tells the story of no ordinary life.

THE ARMY

Whilst the profile of the British Army has been raised through recent conflicts, and the reporting of the tragic deaths and causalities that occur, to many ordinary people the structure and the way it works remains a mystery. If people are to get the most from this short book it will help to have a very basic understanding of how the Army is structured and who does what.

Some nations rely on a very small professional Army, where people volunteer to become full-time career soldiers, but which is bolstered by 'conscription'; that is, people who are made to serve a short time in the military, often between one or two years, before getting on with the rest of their lives. This conscription can also be known as National Service.

Britain has generally always operated a different way, choosing to rely on a professional, but relatively small, full-time Army. Whilst it's hard to imagine, during the years that led up to WW2, the British Army strength stood at about 200,000 men – in context that is only about twice as many people as you can fit in a large modern day sports stadium! By contrast, in 2011, the Army's strength stood at about half this size and is still shrinking.

In Britain, many more soldiers belonged to the Territorial Army (TA), a volunteer reserve, who did their basic training once a week and then had a concentrated period of unit training on a two-week annual camp. These reserve forces could be called on to serve alongside their full-time regular Army colleagues if required to do so.

In WW2, much as you would find today, the Army consisted of teeth arms (or combat units), based around a Divisional / Brigade structure which was hierarchical. A Division was huge (thousands of men and tons of equipment), and would consist of a number of Brigades with each in turn consisting of about 3 Infantry Battalions. Each Battalion was made up of about 4 rifle companies and a headquarters (HQ) Company. The Battalion was usually the biggest formation most soldiers associated with, and to which they felt a true sense of belonging and pride, but it was the Company structure, with about 3 rifle platoons (each consisting of a number of sections of about 8 men) where fighting men did their work forging close bonds with the people on their sections.

A Brigade would also need the support of other 'Arms' and therefore it would have its own Engineers (or Sappers), Transport, Logistics, Medical personnel and Artillery. The Artillery would usually consist of 3 Field Regiments with big guns, split into two batteries. They would provide the fire support that was either planned as part of an operation (we are going to attack at 10pm tomorrow and want a pre-arranged barrage) or on call in case things went wrong (we are in the shit right now and need immediate fire support). In theory, this kind of fire support helped destroy the will of an enemy to fight making it easier to defeat them.

Despite the gentle 'leg-pulling' of some in the Royal Air Force, Royal Navy and Support Arms, any infantryman will tell you that wars are won with 'boots on the ground'. Yes, you need artillery and air support, or naval bombardments, but when it comes down to it, it's nearly always about blokes with determination, aggression, and moral courage who are prepared to confront and kill the enemy.

I would call all of the above regular forces, but there also existed specialist forces who were trained in a different way to do different and difficult things. In today's world, you might know these units as the Parachute Regiment or Royal Marines; these were made up of people who were highly trained and highly fit, where entry into their system was by a tough selection process. During the early years of WW2 their equivalent would have been the Commandos (Army and Royal Marine) and Parachute Brigades.

Finally, there also exists a level above these specialist forces. I am not one who often favours the word elite; in today's world, it seems the term elitism is used to describe a belief that certain people deserve favoured or special treatment by virtue of their perceived privileged superiority.

But speak to any world class athlete who strives to be the best they can be, better than anyone else in the world, and they will paint a very different picture of the word elite. It is therefore in this context that I use the term elite to describe the very small number of servicemen and women who put themselves in frequent danger, doing things of strategic importance, often in small highly secretive self-supporting groups, a long way from home and in the face of immense harm. They are the members of the Special Air Service (SAS) and Special Boat Service (SBS) and many of their traditions, values, training methods and ethos remain the same today as they were in the early days of WW2.

With the death and passing of many WW2 veterans, our links to World War fade. Our knowledge of what the armed forces do is framed by smaller conflicts, fought a long way from home, involving a relatively small number (by WW2 standards) of very brave people. Now imagine that our Country was under threat of invasion from an Army that had raced across Europe with devastating speed and brutality.

This brought war to our doorstep and after the retreat of our Army from Dunkirk, France, our forces were cooped up on our shores unable to deploy or fight back because virtually the whole of Europe was under the shadow of Hitler and his allies. This was war on an enormous scale, that touched every man, woman, child and household. Industry and factories had to re-skill and start producing materials with which war could be fought. Everybody was asked to do their bit – it didn't affect the few, it affected the many. My father's story begins in the early 30's, several years before the outbreak of the War in1939. It starts in Birmingham, England.

REVEILLE – THE VERY BEGINNING

It was always the cold that woke me. In the winter, same time every morning, usually at about 4am. I don't know if it was my chattering teeth or my shivering but despite being squashed between my two brothers, covered in coats and clothes, I still couldn't sleep. I was born on 17th February 1921 and was one of ten children. We lived in a rented two-bedroom Victorian terraced house in Small Heath, Birmingham, in the shadow of Birmingham City football ground, St Andrews. Just pause and imagine that for a second before reading on – ten children and two bedrooms.

The house was gas-lit and furnished with old, battered second-hand furniture. I would never wear underpants (we couldn't afford them), didn't know what a saucer looked like or what it would be used for, never saw a tablecloth and would go to school in winter, shivering with cardboard stuck inside the soles of my shoes to cover the holes.

Our bed was a mattress stuffed with straw, we often had fleas, and my clothes were hand-me-downs that had been worn by my brothers before me. I would never know the feel of new clothes until I was in my late teens, when they were given to me by the Army. By modern standards, we were incredibly poor but despite this, if you looked up or down our street, everyone lived the same way. Therefore, nobody knew that life could be any different and we just thought that this was the way that normal people lived; as a consequence, we never even considered we were really desperately poor. My dad was a manual worker at a large local factory drawing a very modest wage and my mother didn't work (other than bringing up a family of ten!). Living this kind of life instilled in a child the ability to 'stick up' for yourself in a number of ways.

It was the 1930's, a time of great depression falling between the two World Wars; they were the days of the major slump in employment when it was very hard for people to find work and there was also a great deal of poverty. Yet despite benefits being available, it seemed that no one wanted to claim them. It was considered humiliating and socially unacceptable and even in our very poor community, where there were degrees of poverty, everyone wanted to avoid the stigma of benefits.

It's funny how things shape you. During my darkest moments as a Prisoner of War (POW), I often laughed and smiled to myself as I reached back and recalled some of my early memories. It was a fact of life that household jobs got handed down from brother to brother and as I was born the fifth child with three older brothers, Arthur, Leslie and John, I knew my time would come. One day shortly after my twelfth birthday, my mum told me that I would have a new Monday job, taking over responsibility from my brother John.

There was a great love and bond between John and I, which remained until his death in 1985. Both of us owed so much to our school teachers who clearly saw something a little bit different in the two of us. I went to an all-boy's school. They made us see a bigger world and encouraged us, through books and learning, to aim as high as we could. Education was considered a 'way out' of poverty.

I was a fairly bright scholar always in the top stream and in most exams I was usually top or second boy. These were the days when great stress was made of King and Country and every year we had a day off for what was called Empire day when we held street parties and parades. King George V was on the throne and they were the days when the map of the World, which was displayed in every classroom, was dotted everywhere with red, the colour of the British colonies. This was truly an Empire on which the sun never set; everywhere, somewhere the sun was shining, fluttering on the Union Jack. We were genuinely proud of that. Working hard at school paid dividends as both John and I sat and passed entry exams to grammar school but more of this later.

And so it was shortly after my twelfth birthday, just before John moved to Grammar school, I found myself waiting until my dad had gone to work and then being handed a bundle prepared by my mum and walking with John to the pawn shop. This was my new household job! John looked at the pawn broker and handed the bundle over; he nodded at the big bloke behind the counter and said "It's him now". The pawnbroker replied, "so you'll be the new Stokes will you?" and of course I then realised that both my brothers before me had been responsible for the 'Monday bundle'.

Over the following weeks I'd take the bundle, run home to mum with the money and then frantically race to school. Of course, I became routinely late every Monday and after the third Monday of doing this my teacher asked me to stay behind. He asked me why I had suddenly become late every Monday. I couldn't look him in the eye and delivered some really weak excuse about a new baby sister in the family and told him my mum could confirm this but he shouldn't involve my dad.

I couldn't admit that we had no money and needed to pawn our belongings to make ends meet, and that my dad knew nothing about it. To be honest, at the age of twelve I'm not sure I understood either! He asked me whether this would continue every Monday and I said it would. He looked at me and didn't speak for what felt like an age and then said "Stokes, I hope things settle down with your new sister but until then don't disturb the class when you come in on a Monday, just come in and sit straight down". He knew of course.

So as we were growing up we all had jobs: those that were too young to work outside the home were expected to work in the home. I still remember my small tired hands gripping a scrubbing brush as I helped my mother scrub the red brick floor of the living room. I have such vivid memories of that floor and the hearth in the kitchen. You see despite being desperately poor, I would run home from school at lunchtime, and as I stepped into the house I could smell stew cooking in a big black cast-iron pot and I recall my mother dipping a thick slice of freshly cut bread in the yellow fat simmering on the top. What a lunch! It was so hot that I had to shift it from hand-to-hand quickly between bites so I could eat it. It tasted bloody delicious.

It was the practice in small working-class homes with large families that the children would be packed off to bed early so that dad, after a hard day's work, could relax, read his paper and snooze. We didn't have a wireless or a television, or a gramophone. I particularly used to hate being packed off to bed early in the light, long, summer evenings whilst lying listening to the cries of the other children at play in the street below. Every week, however, we children took it in turns to have a 'stopping up' night which was truly cherished. I can remember sitting quietly listening to the slight hiss of the gas mantle and watching dad snoring in the chair while mother worked patching and re-patching our trousers and darning socks which were already a mass of patches. Some nights, on very rare occasions when there was a small amount of spare money, my stopping-up task was to pop down to the off-licence at the bottom of the road and fetch Dad's beer which he loved.

Mostly, however, there was no money; there was never enough money and on stopping-up evenings there was an uneasy atmosphere in the house. Almost everyone was poor but even at that age I realised there were fine degrees of poverty. One of the ways that we knew people were really very poor was when children were given free charity dinners at school. It was always the case that daily, at about 11.30 in the morning, the teacher would call the few boys forward individually and hand out the free ticket which they would hand in at the big hall and receive their charity dinner.

Truth to tell the rest of us always used to feel a little bit superior because we didn't have charity dinners, we were all lucky enough to go home to mum at lunchtime. You can imagine my horror one day, when at 11.30, the master called my name on the free meals list. I went completely scarlet and when I got to his desk I said "Sir, we don't have school dinners, we don't have charity dinners, we go home for dinner" he quietly looked at me and said "Sadly Stokes, from today you do". I didn't know it at the time but this was another impact of Johnny going off to grammar school.

I mentioned that our way of dealing with the situation was the 'bundle' that would go in every Monday to the pawnshop and come out every Saturday as soon as mother had my dad's wages. My dad, of course, knew none of this! The thing of greatest value in that bundle was my dad's one and only suit. He had one night out a week, a Saturday, so he never ever went out after this until the following Saturday so the suit was never missed.

I remember vividly the utter calamity one evening in the middle of the week when my Dad came home early. My mother, her eyes wide open with horror, whispered to me and my brother "I think your dad is going out this evening". This was on a Wednesday night with the suit safely locked in the pawn shop and instead of taking his usual chair he went to the kitchen, where we all washed and bathed, and he started to wash. When my mother asked him whether he was going out he said "yes, I've managed to get into the final at the local bowling club and it's me and another chap in the finals, I only found out this morning".

I cannot describe the terrible, brutal, flaming row that developed when he discovered that his suit was missing and he could not go out. Unfortunately, these things were always happening and the cause was because we had no money. I learnt very quickly that although we were a very tight-knit, loving family, the searing, blistering, frightening rows and arguing were all caused by a lack of money.

I remember reading somewhere once, about a child who lived the sort of life I'm writing about now, his parents died and he was sent to live with an uncle and aunt. The single biggest thing that struck him about his new life was the couple and their family did not argue or fight. They were loving and close-knit and whilst there were occasional 'fights', it struck him that the reason why they were like they were was because they had a little bit more money, not lots more, but just a few extra quid a week more. This meant the difference in happiness and upbringing in a house where arguments were rare. Our house was different.

That's not to say there was a lack of love in our house. Indeed, despite there being a strong rivalry between John and I, we loved each other very much. I was closer to John than anyone else and I was very proud of him when he sat and passed for grammar school. John's place had attracted full grants and so my parents didn't have to pay anything but it was still a huge step because normally, each of the boys would have been expected to start full-time work as early as possible to help bring money into the house.

Sometime later, I also sat the exam and passed but was unable to go because we couldn't afford it, therefore, I had to leave school at 14 for full time work in order to keep money coming in; in those days age 14 was the year in which you could legally leave school to start work. With John at grammar school, my parents couldn't afford to have another child not in work and so John's good fortune was at my expense. In later life John and I laughed about this because it shaped us in different ways; he went into the Royal Air Force at the start of the war and I joined the Army, but never once did either of us regret the way that our lives turned out.

As well as the Monday bundle, from the age of 12, I had been working part-time for a greengrocer called Fred Corbett in a place called Bordesley Green in Birmingham. The hours were Thursday and Friday nights from half past five until eight o'clock, Saturday all-day from 9am until 8pm and Sunday from 9.30am to 12 mid-day. There were several boys that worked there and we all had a good laugh. One of the perks of working on a Sunday was to take sacks of cabbage leaves to various people in posh houses for their pets. The few coppers we got we were able to keep; at least I think we were! As time went by, and as some of the more senior boys left, I became one of the senior boys too which meant I didn't have to work on Sundays, which of course was both a blessing (as I got a lie in) and a curse (as I didn't get the few extra pennies)!

My memories of working at this busy greengrocers are mainly happy ones. I very much enjoyed the hustle and bustle, and during school holidays went out with a lorry driver into the country to collect such things as plums and apples; I was often the envy of the other kids who saw me on the back of that truck driving down country lanes, it felt like a good time to be alive. I'd also been on the lorry to Birmingham Smithfield Market, which was a huge wholesale market in the middle of Birmingham, where we used to load and unload fruit and veg. I was really fascinated by the hustle and bustle of market life, and so it was, when I left school at 14, I started work as full-time 'barrow boy' loading the lorries for a firm in the market called Geo Jackson & Co. It was physically gruelling work, a life of very early mornings, amongst some bloody tough folk, but the sounds and sights of market life have lived with me ever since.

It used to amaze me in later life when people turned up at 9am in the butchers or the greengrocer, that they had little idea that at 4am in the morning people had been trading fish, meat and fruit and then bringing it fresh to their local counter. This became a 'dad' story for my kids because on every occasion we would be shopping together at the local greengrocers on Kingsbury Road, Erdington, I would say ' have you any idea where these apples were at 4am this morning and they would groan 'yes'!

Despite the hard life and young age, my friends and I spent a lot of summer weekends camping along the banks of the River Blythe at a place called Hampton in Arden. As a senior boy I never worked on a Sunday so early on a Saturday after work we would bugger off. We stored our equipment in a barn at a local farm and the farmer called us the 'Good Friday Boys' because we always started camping at Easter. I can often remember pitching the tent with everywhere white over with snow and really freezing. It was about this time that we started to get a sense that all was not well in the World. I remember a couple of us, on late summer evenings after dark, lying flat on the banks of the river watching the searchlights probing for planes which were simulating attacking Birmingham.

It was 1936 and I was nearly 15, and whilst we were too young to know it, these were the years that Hitler was on the rise. I remember there being great talk about his troops occupying the Rhineland, which no one really bothered about because everyone felt it belonged to Germany anyway. Then in 1938 Hitler's troops went on to occupy Austria and I felt all around me the mounting panic as he occupied part of Czechoslovakia.

When he finally occupied the whole of Czechoslovakia, it was obvious to all of us that we were heading for war. It was at this time that the Country appealed for volunteers to join the Territorial (part-time) Army (TA); these were the days before conscription. I remember joining a long queue at Stoney Lane Barracks in Birmingham where I enlisted as gunner in the 121st Field Regiment, Royal Artillery (TA). There was no rhyme or reason why I joined this unit, it was just that they wanted TA volunteers and I was in line. It was now early in 1939 – I was just 18 years old.

The weekends and evenings that followed were spent learning the very basics of soldiering such as handling a weapon and shooting, fieldcraft, map reading and compass work. My training culminated with me spending two weeks under canvas at a place called Dalditch Moor in Devon. I'll never forget it, it was the last two weeks in August 1939.

MARCHING OFF

I packed my kit on a hot Saturday afternoon on 19th August 1939 and then marched in full equipment to the local station. My mum was worried and sensed the building storm was not far away but as we hugged I told her not to be silly and said "don't worry mum I'll be back in two weeks". Little did I know as I was marching away that day that I would never put on civilian clothes again for another six years. The reason for this was that whilst we were away on camp in Devon, Germany invaded Poland and on that day we were all mobilised as regular soldiers in the British Army with Britain declaring war with Germany on 3rd September 1939. I was 18 ½ years old.

Throughout the war, especially when I was a prisoner of war, I had so many times to dream about that last Saturday morning at home before I left to march to the station. My last lunch that Saturday had been sausage and mash; I always told my children that that was the dinner on which I went to war! Sadly for my children many years later, whenever we had sausage and mash I

43

would always say "this is the dinner I went to war on". Eventually of course, as soon as there was any mention we might be having this for dinner my kids would shout, "Dad – we know, ok"!

Whilst I took to soldiering like a duck takes to water, I was bitterly disappointed when it was decreed that no one under the age of 20 would be able to go on active service; this basically meant that anyone under this age would not be permitted to fight. So, I had to leave my unit and couldn't believe it when I was transferred to a half-finished anti-aircraft site in the countryside outside Glasgow. It was during the winter of 1939 to 1940 and I still recall this as being one of the coldest, snowiest, harshest winters ever. I remember someone telling me that it was the coldest for about 45 years. The work was physical and I kept myself busy but we knew that units were being shipped to France every week to prepare to oppose Hitler's forces that had swept across Europe; to be honest for a young fit bloke who had joined to do 'my bit' I felt like I was missing out.

There must have been thousands of young men like me who shared this bravado unlike the old and bold (my grandparents) who had seen the horrors of the First World War and said peace would be the better outcome. I didn't know then of course that war would change my life in a profound way forever, or that I would see so many of my best mates killed, so I suppose you need to be careful what you wish for. I have to say that my early eagerness and young bravado was replaced with a quiet sense of realism, determination and professionalism once I joined the Commandos.

In February 1940 the age limit for active service was dropped from 20 years to 19 years and on my 19th birthday I immediately obtained a transfer back to my original Regiment, 121st Field Regiment Royal Artillery. The Regiment was still forming and training, and it was all a bit chaotic. I really believed that we too would be moved to France at some future point in support of the British Expeditionary Force who were now well established in France, and were meant to be acting as a deterrent to Hitler's forces to prevent them from progressing any further. It has always been a mystery to me why we didn't attack the Germans in those early months of 1940 but we didn't.

I suppose the hope of the British Government at the time was that there was still a chance for peace. However, in early May 1940, we paid a heavy price for this as the Germans launched a devastating sustained attack against Luxembourg and Belgium, and then France.

This led to the Dunkirk miracle (or disaster as we called it in the barrack room) when over 300,000 men were successfully rescued and returned back to England after a frantic retreat to the French coast in an attempt to avoid being captured by the Germans as they raced across France. Imagine if that had happened, the bulk of the British Army taken as prisoners of war in 1940! A flotilla of all kinds of boats brought our soldiers back to England.

Despite the successful evacuation, it meant that France lay undefended and the French surrendered in mid-June 1940. Morale plays such an important part in the minds of soldiers and everywhere you looked morale was very low as we had fled from France in retreat. This didn't last long, however, as it seemed natural to us, and our superiors, that Hitler's next step would be the invasion of England via the English Channel. In response to this we, along with many others, were moved to the South Coast of England to prepare to repel any attempted German invasion. As we moved forward we thought this would be the new front line; we really believed that we would be fighting for our Country, our freedom and our way of life on our own soil.

SPECIAL DUTIES

It was about this time, June 1940, when a notice
appeared on all army notice boards asking for
volunteers to form a new special force for very
hazardous duties; there were some barrack rumours that
this was about the formation of suicide squads to cross
the channel and attack the enemy on the continent but
this was just barrack room bollocks. Most soldiers will
tell you that in the absence of any accurate information
they bloody make things up and before you knew it, we
would be attacking Berlin and bringing Hitler back as a
prisoner of war!

What we could not have known at our level at that time,
was that Winston Churchill, our Prime Minister, had
issued instructions to make the South Coast of England
a 'springboard' to attack the entire length of the
German-occupied coastline; he had demanded offensive
action to restore morale and divert German forces into
some form of defensive posture, no matter how limited.
I suppose this was about restoring some pride and not

adopting a siege mentality from which it becomes so hard to think offensively.

In order to deliver this small scale aggressive offensive action, Churchill asked for a number of raiding units, that were to become 12 Army Commando Regiments, each consisting of about 450 men, to be formed in order to take the war to Germany on foreign soil. Churchill stated that there would be "a hand of steel that would come from the sea to pluck German sentries from their positions" and that they would never know when or where this would happen. The brief was that they wanted these new Commando units to be made up of very tough, courageous, highly trained and determined men, who would be capable of operating independently behind enemy lines, using their own initiative. Of course, I only discovered this much later but had I known this at the time I'm not sure I would have volunteered as it didn't sound like a description of me!

Despite this, one or two of us felt compelled to volunteer as it felt like the right thing to do and I could see the writing on the wall for the next few years. I didn't want to be kicking my heels preparing for an invasion of France that would be a number of years away and the thought of as little bullshit as possible also had its appeal. The weeks passed and during this time the 121st Field Artillery Regiment had been posted to a place called Ballymoney in Northern Ireland and then on to Kilkeel.

When the German invasion of England didn't happen, the Army began re-gearing and re-focussing its efforts more towards large scale amphibious operations with the aim of invading German-occupied France at some future time and this would require us to cross the Channel. However, at this point in time in 1940, D-day was still a very a long way in the future!

As weeks passed I had completely forgotten about putting my name forward to join one of these 'special' units, when like a bolt out of the blue I was interviewed by two quite strange officers and accepted for a new unit that was being formed in Belfast, called Number 12 Commando Regiment. I remember all of this being done with the utmost theatrical secrecy. This new Commando Regiment was being raised with volunteers from units already serving in Northern Ireland.

It was only later I discovered that the two officers were working to specific instructions, looking for specific types of handpicked people who were 'intelligent, young, exceptionally fit, who could demonstrate courage, endurance, initiative, resourcefulness, self-reliance, controlled aggression, marksmanship, an ability to swim, and who could drive and were not prone to air or sea sickness'. I think if you were selecting young men as potential recruits for the Commandos today then this list of skills and qualities might look exactly the same!

The idea, and the reality, was that we were expected to be able to conduct assault landings in the dark, in rough weather and on rocky coasts, in areas where the defences might be weak, or seize and destroy coastal defence installations. We were also trained to penetrate behind enemy lines in small teams, in order to destroy lines of communication, ambush enemy forces or take prisoners, landing by boats or submarines. Furthermore, we were also expected to infiltrate airfields to destroy aircraft. Later in the war it came as no surprise to me that the SAS was to emerge from the officers and NCOs who had been trained in the Commando way, sticking to an original commando ethos.

Each Commando Regiment was similar in size to an Army Battalion, with about 450 men, organised into 75 man Troops with 15 man sections. I joined a section of E Troop, where I met one of the finest officers in the war, with whom I'd serve until his death in September 1943; his name was Philip Pinckney or as we called him PHP (the H stood for Hugh). He was our section commander on E Troop.

We undertook some damned harsh training in Northern Ireland and then crossed over to a training area in Scotland and completed our commando training at a place known as Achnacarry on the banks of the river Arkaig in Lochaber. In later life this would become known as Castle Commando. It was here, in Scotland, during the next few months that we broke nearly every British Army record for endurance, marching and shooting, which included things like marching 64 miles in 24 hours, in full kit, in appalling weather conditions.

We were taught to live off the land and I think PHP had known what we were in for because before leaving Northern Ireland we spent a lot of time in the mountains and glens. We marched using a technique which allowed us to move at great speed on direct compass bearings at about 6 miles an hour in full kit, which was fine except sometimes difficult obstacles would get in the way that we were expected to just deal with. Whilst anyone could volunteer for the Commandos, the selection process was extremely tough and a number of blokes were returned to their units (RTU'd) which carried no shame.

Later on, the business of sending blokes home also acted as a significant motivational tool. You can imagine, having become part of a 'family', that the worst thing in the world would be to do something so bad that you might be sent back to your unit. The flip side of this was that occasionally, after an operation, or during really arduous training, some blokes decided that this way of life was not for them and they were just quietly moved on.

In Scotland we were out for weeks on end, mostly at night and it was here that I really learnt to handle boats, how to fire a wide variety of weapons, how to use a 'fighting knife' and kill quickly and silently, and my stock in trade - explosives. Darkness was our daylight and we became completely proficient in operating at night completely in the dark. We were encouraged and trained to be self-reliant, and to use our own initiative to get the job done. There was not the usual sort of divide between officers and men, it was all far more 'all of one company'.

PHP took this to another level as he was not one for bullshit; he allowed us to wear what we needed to wear according to what it was we were doing. This was of course completely at odds with how the 'normal' army operated and sometimes it didn't win friends with senior officers. However, because of things like this, we began to earn a bit of a reputation for being one of the toughest and most effective sections in the Commando.

It might sound far-fetched but we were like Olympic athletes having spent weeks on end over the mountains, day and night, rain and snow, wind and hail. One vivid memory I have of this time was spending six weeks, where the weather was beautiful, on the Island of Skye learning mountaineering in the Cuillin Hills, living off the land, trapping rabbits and shooting deer. We stayed miles away from anywhere in a shooting lodge called Camasunary.

Being a city boy I had no idea how bloody hard it was to stalk a deer but I suppose, as I looked into the future, I realised that the things I was learning were probably going to help preserve my life for as long as possible. There was, therefore, an incentive to be the best you could possibly be.

At this time we spent so many nights practising landings in the Outer Hebrides; some went well and some went so badly that you had to laugh. But it was over these hard, sometimes gruelling, months that a very deep sense of comradeship and a terrific pride in our superb physical fitness and toughness began to emerge. It wasn't elitism; it was just the knowledge that we were to be classed amongst the finest soldiers in the world.

In March 1941, our Commando Regiment (12 Commando) moved to Canterbury, preparing for Operation Barbaric (a major assault on the French coast), which was at first delayed and was then thankfully cancelled at the last minute. There is one thing being the best but quite another being sacrificed and all of us felt like this would be a suicide mission; I admit I had huge sense of relief when it was called off. Churchill himself came to tell us the news that the operation had been cancelled.

It was this kind of thing that was a regular feature of Army life; it's on, it's off, then it's on, then it's off again. One had to learn to cope with the frequent mental and physical preparations for operations that were cancelled, rescheduled and then cancelled again. Although Operation Barbaric was a full Commando raid, the main concept of 12 Commando, unlike other Commando Regiments, was that it had been set up to operate in smaller groups and designed on the basis of raiding in small teams who could carry out reconnaissance, capture and bring back prisoners for interrogation, or gather intelligence.

SMALL-SCALE RAIDING FORCE AND LOFOTEN

It was at this time, in July 1941, that a small detachment of us, led by PHP , travelled to a place called Burlesdon on the River Hamble. As with a lot of things we did, we didn't know what lay ahead or what we were meant to be doing until the very last minute which was for reasons of complete operational secrecy. Therefore, when we set off from Scotland and boarded a train South from Spean Bridge, via Glasgow, we had no idea where we were going.

I really took the village of Burlesdon to heart and it was a place that we were to return to again and again; it lay midway between Southampton and Portsmouth, on the South Coast of England. Someone had decided that an element of our Commando would be allocated part of the French coast that we could raid at will, to take the fight to the Germans. We made our way to a place called Warsash at the mouth of the River Hamble where we were kitted out.

The word raiding would confuse most people today because they couldn't picture what was meant by this. Just imagine an inky black night, wind and rain lashing the French coast. A small concrete command post that inside is warm and well lit with blacked out windows, filled with laughter and the smell of coffee, and cigarettes. The banter between a German gun battery commander and his small command post staff, with talk of home and life in Berlin. A door opens and one of the soldiers slings his rifle over his shoulder and wraps his coat against the biting wind. He goes to the bushes for a piss and when he is finished, peers out at the darkness and wishes he was home. In an instant, his head is jerked back and a fighting knife severs his wind pipe and artery. He dies quietly just before hell is unleashed on this very tiny spot on the French coast resulting in explosive charges being laid and the command post destroyed. This is what raiding was about.

Whilst at Burlesdon, we were out from dark until dawn practising landings on the Isle of Wight. We all lived in different civilian houses and paid our own board and we used to meet during the day outside the village hall. We learnt to handle every small craft imaginable from small canoes, and Falboats to large Motor Torpedo Boats (MTBs). It was also whilst here we were all nearly killed in a ridiculous incident.

Any Commando would tell you that maintaining your range of skills and fitness at a peak and keeping your kit in tiptop condition, took time, effort and energy. Firing your weapon, clearing a stoppage or knowing how to switch quickly between a rifle, or machine gun and a fighting knife, or pistol, were things that would save your life. They needed to be practised constantly. As part of keeping our shooting skills up to scratch we used to do some live firing training in a local quarry. Christ knows what the locals thought.

Anyway, one day we were doing shooting practice and throughout the day had heard our fighters reassuringly patrolling the sky overhead. At the end of shooting practice we were standing near the quarry when one of the aircraft made a very low pass and we took the piss by aiming at the pilot and pretending to fire. Imagine our shock when the bastard opened fire and it was only then we saw the German crosses on the wings. The pilot released his bombs and we dived for cover with the bombs missing us and exploding in the orchard blowing the windows out of the local houses. We just lay on the ground and laughed. I've no doubt that we all looked absolutely ridiculous.

The locals must have thought us mad as sometimes, if we were returning from a long exercise, we used to walk back along the railway line using a high bridge to cross the River. PHP would order everyone to jump in, in full kit, from the highest point and swim to the edge of the river, often assisted by hand grenades dropped into the water to add a bit of realism!

Then one morning we were all asked to assemble in a field across from the village hall and PHP spoke to us, he said "after all the training we have been doing, some of you may have guessed that were are about to undertake the real thing; we are carrying out a raid on the French coast tonight". The raid was to be against a small French coastal town called Ambleteuse on the 27th / 28th / 29th July 1941 - it was codenamed Operation Chess.

A few of us were selected to take part and one of my close mates, Tim Robinson, (known as Robbie) and me were on the raid. It was meant to be a reconnaissance or 'recce' for intelligence gathering purposes. We went to Dover and boarded the Landing craft (LC) at about 22.00hrs and by the light of a candle we blackened our faces using burnt cork. We were towed across the Channel by a motor launch and there were two Landing Craft; we were in the first and a small reserve of about 5 naval personnel were in the other (whose job it would be to 'fire like mad') to cover our return if the things didn't go as planned.

We were 'slipped' about one mile out and made our own way to the objective. PHP, myself and five others went ashore in complete silence with Tim Robinson and others remaining in our Landing Craft. We were ashore for about twenty minutes when all hell broke loose - flares, machine gun fire, and mortars (which thankfully were inaccurate). Then we realised that whilst we were taking some accurate incoming fire, the landing craft was coming under intense cross fire from a fixed machine gun position.

It was clear that the Landing Craft couldn't return fire for fear of hitting us ashore which meant we were not going to get home without first dealing with the machine gun post. PHP and I managed to get under the position and then assault it, putting several grenades into the strong point killing most of the Germans and silencing the position which allowed us to get back to the Landing Craft, by wading as fast as we could up to our necks in the water. Everything was still lit by flares but we were no longer coming under effective enemy fire. It was only later we learnt that Commander Gould (in charge of the boats) wanted to pull out and leave us but his stoker had been hit and died instantly and in the delay Tim Robinson spotted us moving back to the boats.

I still don't know how all of us in the raiding party survived but when we got back to the Landing Craft, it was obvious that someone else on board had been hit and they were in terrible pain. Robbie was trying to fix him up and said he had been hit by a tracer round in the back. I looked after the blokes and PHP, helped by Robbie, gave the casualty morphine but the wound was fatal. He died before we reached England.

It was only later I learned that it was Commander Sir Geoffrey Congreve (Distinguished Service Order) who PHP had tried to save. I'll never forget the sounds of him dying in dreadful agony as we made our way back to Dover. For anyone that thinks war is glamorous try spending the night with a man dying in such a way knowing there is nothing that can be done to save him. Despite this, the night passed without further incident until first light at about 05.00hrs when some navy bloke realised that, due to a compass malfunction, we were still only 3 miles off the coast of France! Imagine that – we had been ashore, assaulted what felt like a German Company, and made it back to our landing craft only to be told we were still only 3 miles from the enemy coastline!

It was only later that I was to discover that the compass problem was a common fault which, at that time, had an unknown cause. It didn't take long to learn that it had something to do with demagnetising ships to protect them from German sea mines that were almost impossible to spot. We just assumed that the Navy couldn't navigate.

Thank God we were spotted and picked up and escorted back to Dover. PHP was asked to nominate a few names for a mention in dispatches but he submitted the whole bloody section and I think the Army senior commanders took it as a bit of a joke but his point had been made. It was about the whole team not any one person and this was how it was to be for the rest of my war. That was my first ever taste of being under enemy fire, a long way from home, with no one else to rely on but yourself, your mates and your equipment.

These ad hoc raids continued but by December 1941, the whole concept of carrying out small raids was becoming far more organised and the combined operations headquarters decided to promote a number of major raids. It was decided that the whole of our Commando Regiment would re-form and launch an attack against the Lofoten Islands, off the coast of German held Norway and about 100 miles north of the Arctic Circle; our part in this was to undertake a diversionary raid known as Operation Anklet. So, for Anklet, we returned to our Regiment and the whole unit was moved to Scapa Flow which was a great naval anchorage off the northern tip of Scotland.

OPERATION ANKLET

We were moved on to two commando carriers under the command of Lt Col Harrison, the commanding officer of our Commando. It was here that we joined quite a large convoy of other warships including the cruiser Arethusa. We had been trained in arctic war fighting and we were issued with arctic fighting equipment including all-white clothing and skis. A few of us, mostly explosive experts, were then transferred to a ship called HMS Bedouin which was a tribal class destroyer.

We sailed the next morning in a force nine gale and I don't ever remember being so miserable, constantly seasick, wet and cold. The North Sea in midwinter, lashed by gales, snow, and dark for most of the time, was a terrible place. Conditions on a destroyer were very poor and normally cramped but add a squad of Commandos and it was bloody ridiculous; it made me remember why I didn't join the Navy!

One morning a sailor who had been chatting to me told me to go on deck and have a look at the sun "you better look at that mate" he said "because you won't be seeing it again until we come back across the Arctic Circle - today we cross it going North and we are sailing into darkness". I went on deck and looked towards the horizon, the sun came up and over and vanished in about two hours and that was it from that point on - we were in the dark permanently. The timing of this operation (in permanent darkness) had something to do with us being too far north for our own air cover and if we did it in the dark, the ships were less likely to be bombed! This worried me a little bit because I didn't want to die sitting in a tin can feeling really sick, and I longed to get off and do my job with my feet on 'terra firma'.

It was at this point, where we had reached the point of no return, that we were briefed on the mission in detail. The job of our small detachment was to land and blow up the communications cable connecting the islands and destroy other key installations. We landed on the westerly island of Moskenesoy at 6:00am on Boxing Day morning, 26th of December 1941. Can you imagine how we felt on Christmas Day, preparing charges, checking weapons and thoroughly checking kit not knowing if we were going to see 1942. Happy Christmas!

As it turned out we made a completely unopposed landing at a tiny village at the head of the fjord where, waist deep in snow we set about laying explosive charges to destroy the communications cable. It was a mystery to me why there was no German detachment guarding it. They were certainly about, as the sound of heavy gunfire came to us as the main assault went in. It was only some time later that we learnt the reason for such little German resistance was that they had all been enjoying Christmas a little too much, and had not been expecting a visit from us on Boxing Day.

After blowing up the cable and main buildings, we returned to the destroyer which was later joined by two others. The three flew German flags and carried out a sweep of a place called Narvik Fjord. It was here that they stopped one ship which was boarded and they found six German officers just going home to Germany on leave - imagine that, what poor luck for them! We spent the next two days destroying installations before we were ordered back home and I have some happy memories of being made very welcome in the tiny simple Norwegian cottages but I was not sad to leave the dark, bleak, mountain fjord's and that sense of a long, bleak winter.

Part of me did wonder what would become of the locals once we had buggered off and Hitler's forces had reoccupied the area. Despite this, we learned later that our raid, and the main attack, had had the desired affect and forced Hitler to divert significant forces to defend the Baltic and Norwegian Coastlines as they were not able to rule out that these Coasts would be where a major force would land to commence the fight to recapture mainland Europe.

A short time after returning back to the UK, a handful of us were transferred with PHP to a place called Churston Manor (Lupton), midway between Brixham and Dartmouth on the South Coast of England. The move came about as we had been asked to make up the numbers of men who'd been killed on Number One Small-Scale Raiding Force (1 SSRF) which had been under the command of a Major Gus March-Phillipps. March-Phillipps had also been killed on the raid in France and the unit was now commanded by Major Geoffrey Appleyard who had been his second in command.

We were based in a beautiful manor house, in an isolated valley which became a residential boy's school after the war. We had our own motor torpedo boat (MTB 344) based on the River Dart and we were allotted a section of the enemy coast to raid when, where and how we saw fit in order to take prisoners, gain intelligence and destroy key targets.

It was whilst serving with the SSRF that I travelled to a place called Ringwood, near Manchester, to complete my parachute training at Number 1 Parachute Training School (PTS). This involved amongst other things jumping through mock aircraft doors onto matting and being suspended from some sort of scaffolding whilst being descended at various speeds. After some ground training we moved onto a series of live jumps. Parachuting was in its infancy and still being developed, it all felt a bit ad hoc but was effective and exhilarating. It was here that I leant a phrase that remained with me all my life which was 'he who hesitates is lost'. This simply meant that if you had to jump, then you had to jump, refusing only made it twice as hard the next time and the time after that. A number of blokes did refuse, which was probably no bad thing as the last thing you wanted when jumping behind enemy lines with a party or 'stick' of ten men, was someone deciding at the last minute they didn't like heights!

Not everyone in the Army was happy about what we were doing regarding raiding; some saw it as a complete waste of time and resources, some saw it as being maverick and some a threat. Our original Commanding Officers (in my case back at the 121st Royal Artillery) were obviously pretty annoyed at losing some of their top blokes to these special units that were cloaked in secrecy. It's worth mentioning that despite nearly all of my entire war service being spent with the Commandos, SSRF and the SAS, my personal records were always held with my original Regiment, the Royal Artillery. This meant that you stayed on their unit strength and never appeared, for record purposes, as being part of any of the other units. This was to be a big help when I was taken prisoner of war.

OPERATION BASALT - THE RAID ON SARK
SEPTEMBER / OCTOBER 1942

Despite all the raiding that we did, it was one of the
smaller raids with 1 SSRF that we were remembered
for; it was called Operation Basalt which was originally
planned for the nights of 19th / 20th September. The
raid was to be mounted by a small number of men,
including Major Appleyard, PHP, a young Danish
officer called Anders Lassen, and few of our Troop.
We were to cross in our MTB landing on one of the
Channel Islands called Sark, a really tiny British island
that is miles from England situated just off the coast of
Normandy, France.

The Channel Islands had been occupied by German
forces from the summer of 1940. The main purpose of
the mission was to take prisoners and get them back to
England for questioning about German defences along
the French coast and the state of their equipment and
morale.

We were to leave Portland by motor torpedo boat on Saturday 19th September, as long as the weather conditions were right. The moon played such a big part in our operations and on the night of 19th September the moon would rise and then set at about 1.30am in the early hours of the morning. This meant we had enough light for the operation whilst the moon was up and waning, with darkness and an overcast sky to cover our extraction and return.

We left Portland at about 10.00pm and around midnight sighted land and reduced engine speed to silent running but it was quickly established we were off course. These sort of fuck-ups happened all of the time. We altered course and about 20 minutes later approached the Island of Sark, our target. We navigated around the Island to our departure point which we reached at about 01.30am when the engines were cut.

Our life was operating out of small boats so we knew how to read the weather and the sea, and on this occasion we could sense a number of things that didn't feel right. There was a strong wind, very strong current and big swell. Simply to get into a position from which we could get ashore would have taken us until about 3am and we knew that we needed to have the operation completed and be heading home at 03.30hrs.

Major Appleyard told us all quietly that we would need to cancel the operation and so we made our way back to Portland arriving at 05.30hrs. This was how it was sometimes, in fact more often than not, and if you are going to risk the lives of men then it takes as much courage to abort an operation as it does to give the thumbs up and to proceed with it.

We were debriefed and then made our way back to our billets. On 26th September Major Appleyard requested that the operation be re-mounted by MTB, using the same plan and methods, on the 3rd / 4th October when the moon and tides would be right. The operation was approved.

We assembled in Portland again on 3rd October and left by MTB 344 at around 19.20hrs. By 21.30hrs we had arrived off the Island of Sark with a good sea and good weather conditions. By 22.20hrs we were in position 4 miles due East off the southern tip of the island. We approached really cautiously until we were just off the rocks and the MTB dropped anchor. We had been briefed that we would come ashore at one of two places, either Dixcart Bay or Derrible Bay. However, air reconnaissance reports had told us that a new fixed machine gun position had been sighted on top of the steep cliffs, near a place called the Hogs Back, which we were told had been sighted to cover the two small beaches in each of the bays. Apart from these two tiny beaches there was only one other place that we might have been able to get ashore on the Island.

Dixcart Bay offered an easy landing point with a valley sweeping inland, whereas Derrible Bay was a very small beach that could only be used as a landing point at high tide which had to be followed by a great big climb up sheer cliffs with full kit. This was by far the more the difficult approach and we had worked out that it was virtually impossible for a machine gun position to fire directly into the bottom of the cliffs. This was the way we would go, taking us up onto a very narrow ridge called Hogs Back that would lead inland to our target area.

We left the MTB at just after 23.00hrs to row ashore with Anders Lassen sculling. Unfortunately we landed on a rocky outcrop with a couple of us going ashore and realising we were not on the mainland. We both swam across to the main landing point and the others sculled in, helped by the two of us who were now ashore. Lieutenant Young stayed with the boat. All you could hear was the wind and the noise of the sea. The rest of us set off up the sheer 150 foot cliff making our way slowly towards the top of the Hogs Back; it was a very difficult climb that eased towards the top. What we thought might be a tough scramble was a full climb and really hard work. Anders Lassen had been sent to do 'recce' of the ridge line and Hogs Back, to find out where the machine gun post was sighted but he soon returned and told us that the intelligence had been wrong and there was no such position. This was good news as we would either have had to deal with it quietly or go around it.

As it was, the route inland was pretty rough going through really thick prickly gorse and bracken, and we reached our first objective just after 1am, which turned out to be some disused cottages that we thought might

79

be occupied. From here we moved off to a very large house with out- buildings where a small party of three went forward to do a recce and then everyone else was called forward. It was the home of La Dame de Sark who told us where to find the Germans; it appeared that they were at about platoon strength or about 25 / 30 blokes (there were about 11 of us). We also learned from her that a number of locals were being shipped to mainland German labour camps. She gave us maps of the island and very detailed information about where the German troops were located. She was offered the chance to return with us to England but declined and said this was her home and she wanted to stay. As things turned out it was a bloody good job she stayed in the house.

Although time always flashed by as you were living on your nerves and adrenalin, in reality we had now been ashore for a long time. We were told that one of the party was going to leave us and make their way back to the coast in order to signal the boat and let them know we were ok as we didn't want them buggering off without us. The Germans were in split locations at the Dixcart Hotel but the closest billet, where they were sleeping, was the hotel annexe. Quick orders were delivered and everyone knew their drills. We searched the place and found five sleeping German soldiers. As we roused them there was a dawning realisation that they were going to be taken prisoner. We took everything that was going to be of intelligence value and headed outside where a number of people had been covering the approaches. As we were securing the prisoners, one of the Germans made a break for it and suddenly chaos ensued with a serious scuffle and he was shot; two more prisoners tried to escape and raise the alarm. Up to this point in the raid we had managed to be relatively stealthy not wanting to start a war with the other 25 German soldiers billeted in close proximity.

Years after the war I have had time to reflect on these moments and situations like this are rarely understood by anyone who has never been in such a position. We were by now a small team of ten men, a long way from home on an enemy held Island miles away from our only transport facing a far superior force.

Anyone who has handled prisoners under combat conditions a long way from home on the enemy's doorstep will know how hard this is. Especially when your prisoners know that you are outnumbered and outgunned, and that their lives are about to change forever one way or another. People can react to this in many different ways, some are subdued, which is what you hope for, others you know will fight. Once all hell breaks loose there is only one way to deal with this and it's to be aggressive and controlling right from the start. It's known as the shock of capture. You can't fuck about.

Our job wasn't to fight the whole Island, our mission was to get prisoners home alive. By now everyone was being alerted to our position and we had only seconds in which to decide what to do. In the chaos two more German soldiers were killed leaving two who we were going to take back to England. Both of these men had been properly restrained with their hands tied. One of them was completely subdued the other struggled wildly in response to the loud and approaching sounds of his fellow comrades who were now heading in our direction.

We were told to bugger off and make haste back to the boat. I moved towards the front of the party with two us forcibly taking control of the first POW. What seemed like a few seconds later we heard an almighty ruckus behind us and another shot was fired. We managed to recover one of the prisoners (*Obergefreiter Weinrich*) safely back to England where he provided a great deal of information. We made it back to the MTB at about 03.45hrs and as we made our escape, the Island was lit by lights and flares and we could now hear the sound of gunfire (not coming in our direction); we made our way safely back to Portland. I think they thought they were being invaded. Left behind were two Commando knives, a Sten machine gun magazine, a pistol, a pair of wire cutters, torches, a woollen cap, a scarf and several toggle ropes.

It was shortly after this that Hitler, who had been infuriated by our actions, decided to issue his Kommandobefehl (Commando Order) on 18 October 1942 stating that all Commandos, in uniform or not, would be shot dead on sight whether we were taking part in an operation or escaping. Later in the war, a number of my very best friends would pay the ultimate price for our raid on Sark, being shot without question, but we were not to know this at the time.

This made me very angry for number of years after the war because whilst we may have been tough, ruthless and bloody violent when we needed to be, none of us could have ever executed an unarmed man in cold blood, which is what Hitler had implied for propaganda purposes. At least one man had been shot with his hands restrained but I was unaware of this until we made it back to the boat. The implication that he had been executed was utter bollocks. We were too well trained and disciplined to behave like uncontrolled savages and undisciplined thugs.

NORTH AFRICA AND THE BEGINNING OF 2ND SAS

So it was after several small successful raids we found ourselves in late October / early November 1942, moved to the Clyde in Scotland where we boarded a troop ship, which became part of the huge joint amphibious task force of thousands of men that sailed in the middle of the night bound for North Africa.

PHP had heard of the plans to form the 2nd Special Air Service (SAS) and he asked four of us to join him and Major Appleyard, with some of the other Small Scale Raiding Force troops, to set up 2nd SAS in North Africa. We became part of Operation Torch, the First Army's invasion of Algiers. The operation was under the command of a general who was unknown to us at the time, an American named General Eisenhower. The reason we were under American command was this was the first time we were to operate with US Forces who had not long joined our war.

You may recall that only a small number of men from 12 Commando reinforced the SSRF for the raid on Sark. Shortly after this, however, the SSRF was significantly expanded with more soldiers from 12 Commando. This much larger unit, now about 120 strong, required a more senior commander and Lieutenant Colonel Bill Stirling, the brother of David Stirling (of 1 SAS), was placed in charge; Major Appleyard became his Operations Officer. When the time came to deploy to Africa, however, Pinckney ordered only a handful of his 12 Commando men to deploy with him which must have been bitterly disappointing for those left behind. Shortly after this, 12 Commando was disbanded and the men dispersed amongst other units.

The reason behind the decision to deploy the SSRF to North Africa was that the English Channel, and French Coast, was slowly being closed to small scale raiding. With no future role in sight, Stirling took the decision to deploy PHP and Anders Lassen to Africa to support 1 SAS. The plan was that this would lead to a hearts and minds campaign supporting the formation of 2nd SAS[1].

The British Eighth Army had been fighting in North Africa and Egypt since late 1941 but the invasion of Morocco, Tunisia and Algeria (Operation Torch) was probably the first combined major land-sea-air offensive of WW2. The USA entered the war in December 1941 after Hitler had declared war on America. Despite this, it appeared to take several months for US forces to be committed to our war in Europe. Operation Torch was, therefore, the first huge joint undertaking and the job of the combined UK/US joint Eastern Task Force, to which we had been assigned, was to secure Algeria. The idea was to surprise Hitler's Axis powers and occupy North Africa, using it as a springboard to then invade Italy. It was hoped that the Eighth Army and First Army would 'squeeze' the Axis forces in North Africa, at Cape Bon, in the same way that the Germans had done to our British Forces at Dunkirk.

Algeria has a short coastline, about 600 miles, and a land mass of about 900,000 square miles (compared to the UK at about 152,000 square miles). It was a vast Country. We had a virtually unopposed landing to the east of Algiers which turned out to be a bit of a fuck up. Despite this, for me personally these were heady and very exciting days. I know it sounds daft but here I was, a kid from Small Heath in Birmingham, suddenly in North Africa. I loved Algeria, you could come out of rugged rocky mountains into valleys filled with ripe corn and orange groves, and here and there an old French colonial house. At nightfall, after driving all day, our jeeps would lager up in a circle and we would sleep under the trucks being woken to do a two-hour stretch of guard duty. The absolute peace and quiet, the smell of the African desert, the night full of such amazing stars, but always knowing there was every chance that we would run into the advance force of the Germans who were racing towards us in order to keep us out of Tunisia.

And so it was that after some uneventful days and nights we reached a point where reports were coming in hourly of contact being made in various places with the enemy. Our jeeps were equipped with mounted twin Vickers machine guns and as a group of blokes we had already been together through some pretty serious fighting. I say this because our first engagement of the campaign was a bit of a cock-up to be honest, a bit like ending up 3 miles off the French coast when we should have been in Dover - but that's war! We moved in to do a tactical reconnaissance of a small village that sat astride the road. Someone muttered unconvincingly that they thought they had seen the flash of a vehicle on the other side of the village, which we knew couldn't be one of ours.

We knew our 'drills' and with our senses on full alert, we drove around the village and across a sandy patch of scrub when, just in time, we spotted a German armoured car traversing his main weapon to open fire on us. We both opened fire at the same time with his first round missing but by then we were sending some pretty heavy machine gun fire in his direction. Our jeep made a sharp about turn and we buggered off pretty quickly, being hit in several places, as the village was now crawling with Germans. I'll explain in a minute why we buggered off and didn't stand and fight.

Later we laughed about how incredibly lucky we had been, and that was the way it was sometimes, you had to laugh because laughing was our way of coping. It was a black humour that others who had not been in that position, time and again, could never really understand. My brothers later in life would ask, 'how could you laugh at being shot at'? This is one of those questions that if you have to ask then you just wouldn't understand the answer so there is really no point in trying to explain.

We pushed East towards Tunisia, and in the same way that I loved Algeria, some of the places in Tunisia have stayed with me all my life particularly Medjez El Bab, Sousse and the port of Tebarka. We saw some short periods of tough fighting as we made our way towards Tebarka but our job, as recce forces, was not to engage and kill the enemy it was to probe and find out where they were, and their strengths and weapons, which we could then report back. The idea of this was to allow the HQ to build a picture of enemy forces so they knew where best to commit our main force attack (or sometimes where not to attack).

And then one day, in early Spring 1943, a few of us were given the order to pull back from the front line and we were told to report to an area just outside the small port of Philippville, now under our control, which lay on a bay overlooked by low hills on the north eastern coast of Algeria. On arrival we were reunited with Major Appleyard (who was by now appointed second in command of our new unit) and PHP, and told that we would indeed be helping to form the 2nd SAS. As predicted back in England, 2 SAS was to be commanded by Lieutenant Colonel Bill Stirling.

Over the next few days I would help to pitch the first few tents that would become our new base camp and I met a number of senior NCO's who had come across from 1st SAS, who were serving with the Eighth Army. They had been sent to give us the benefit of their experience, and they certainly did! It was very early 1943.

We quickly learned from PHP that Stirling's philosophy was to use us strategically, operating in small groups of 4 / 8 blokes landing by boat, air or submarine, mainly at night, to gain intelligence, take prisoners or destroy key installations and disrupt enemy operations.

The methods of operating were natural to those of us who had worked as part of the SSRF. It was nothing we hadn't done before and I was pretty used to the boat work, explosives, unarmed combat, navigation and parachuting. There were also a few of us there who already knew what it was like to operate in small groups, in close combat, a long way from home. Major Appleyard knew us personally and knew we were bloody good soldiers who were physically and mentally tough.

It was to be from Philipville over the next few months that we were to mount several raids, some that were successful and some that were a complete farce but we would always return to this base for a short period of rest. I remember one of the early raids where I was one of a party of eight, with Major Appleyard in charge, where we were put ashore on Lampedusa, the largest of the Pelagie Islands half way between Tunisia and Sicily.

After about four nights march we were to carry out attacks on petrol installations. Of course the whole essence of the operation was that the enemy were not meant to know that we had landed. It was decided that we would be taken by two motor torpedo boats (MTBs), towing our very small and very serviceable wooden boats called Dorys. We had used these a lot when we were with the SSRF so it was business as usual for us. We were then to paddle ashore and attack the petrol installations and recover back to the motor torpedo boats.

Anyway, a truck took us to the port of Tebarka, which was in absolute ruins and completely shattered; as we sat waiting every so often there was a terrific explosion and rumble that shook the ground as a shell landed which had been fired by long-range German artillery. After dark we assembled on the quay with Major Appleyard and we boarded our two MTBs. Sometime later, at the appointed launch point, in the middle of the night, we transferred to the small wooden Dory's and paddled quietly to shore.

Bear in mind that when you went ashore you had everything you needed to do the job and fight a small war. Consequently our rucksacks weighed about 65lbs each (that's over 5 stones). Every man had drills to perform and we all new our place and what our actions would be in various situations as we had thought through what could happen and rehearsed each situation as much as we could. If all else failed we were trained to just use our skills and initiative.

Often, one of the most tricky parts of the operation was getting ashore. On this occasion, while still a long way from the shore the boat grounded. Major Appleyard climbed out of the boat and started prodding in front of him with the boathook to find the depth whilst we scanned the shoreline. Suddenly, he bloody vanished under the water and into the gloom. One of the skills you had to have was to be a very strong swimmer, which was just as well as a few moments later he appeared again soaking wet and told us we had hit a sand bar. We all knew the drill and got out of the boat and shouldered our rucksacks. The Dory now rode high with us and the rucksacks no longer in it. Suddenly the sand bar disappeared and we were now pushing the fucking boat up to our necks in water.

We continued and were now only a few metres from the shore with the water at ankle height. At that moment all hell broke loose as 3 separate machine gun positions simultaneously opened fire. These things could fire about 600 rounds per minute and the sound of incoming fire shattered what had been the peace and stillness of the night. We were too far away to assault any of the positions and our mission was already compromised so we had to bugger off pretty quickly.

We rushed the boat back into the water and jumped in completely forgetting that the damned thing wouldn't float and it grounded again. We needed to dump our rucksacks push like mad, jump in and row for our lives back to the waiting MTBs. Quite how we survived is a mystery to me. And that was that, a complete fucking fiasco. We headed back to Tebarka, cold, soaking wet and minus our kit which was now at the bottom of the Mediterranean Sea. We arrived back in Tabarka and spent the rest of the night in the shell of what remained of the Hotel Mimosa a shattered two-storey building. We waited for another three days at which point Major Appleyard cancelled the raid and we headed back to Philippville with our tails between our legs. I mention it just to show that sometimes things just went completely wrong, not just a bit wrong, and I remember thinking, not for the first time, that it would be a miracle if any of us were going to make it through the war.

There were of course moments of light relief. I remember us returning back to Philippville after an operation and when we arrived back we found that the last intake of officers for SAS selection and training had arrived, and they were all from the Guards. You need to remember that we were pretty battle hardened by this stage and must have looked like a rag tag lot. Whilst we had been away there had been a general tightening of discipline at the main camp, which was huge, and it was just the sort of thing that really pissed us off.

Can you believe this meant that officers and sergeants sitting down to dinner had to dress formally in a shirt and tie? We thought this was just bloody ridiculous as we were there resting between operations, consequently we spent most of our time in shorts. In the Sergeants' Mess we were accepted and indulged for what we were, seasoned veterans doing difficult things, and so despite the odd frown from the Regimental Sergeant Major, we were left alone.

It was, however, very different in the Officers' Mess where a number a very new 'pukka' young Guards subalterns took a very dim view about the 'eccentric' attire of PHP. Of course, this placed the Officers' Mess hierarchy in a very difficult position because our reputation, especially that of Captain Pinckney, was pretty legendary. Indeed, PHP was known and admired across the whole of Special Operations. We found all of this highly amusing.

The solution was that the Camp Adjutant was told to have a quite word in PHP's ear and called him to one side and after apologising said "the Colonel's compliments but he has noted general standards are slipping and has requested would you mind wearing a tie to dinner tonight". Later in the day PHP of course told us about this and we said "well, that's it you're buggered". He replied that he had already given it a lot of thought and he asked us to tactically conceal ourselves outside the Mess later that evening.

We watched as Officers started arriving for diner in all their finery, the Mess got fuller and fuller but still no sign of Pinckney. Eventually when everyone had arrived and was seated along he came and entered the Mess stark bollock naked except for a neck-tie! There was a moments stunned silence and then the whole Mess erupted in laughter. He sat and ate his dinner in just a tie and the next day a new order was issued that all officers were to dress for dinner with the exception of Captain Pinckney of 2 SAS!

I mention this because one minute you could be fighting for your life behind enemy lines and the next transported to the surreal environment of normality with routine orders and dressing for dinner. I often found this sort of thing really funny.

Ambletuese France – Operation Chess

MTB 344 – courtesy of Chris Rooney

Stokey aged 18 in 1939

Anderson Manor

SSRF Dory Drills – courtesy of Chris Rooney

99   SARK. — Derrible Bay and Point. — La Baie et la Pointe Derrible. — LL.

Sark Landing site – Operation Basalt

Lampedusa

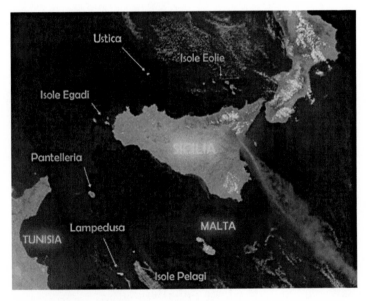

Lampedusa, Pantellaria and Sicily

HMS Unshaken

Stokey 2nd SAS 1944

Horace and Joan Stokes

Father and son - 1984

STEPPING STONES TO ITALY - PANTELLERIA

A short time later, in early May 1943, the Germans and Italians surrendered (about 250,000 of them) in Cape Bon, North Africa. We were briefed that the next main allied objective would be Sicily and then hopefully on to Italy giving us a toe hold back in Europe where we could open a front and push the Germans back. This meant that the main body of the Army in Africa could rest and prepare for Sicily which was a couple of months away. In the meantime we were told that there were a number of Islands that lay in the Med that would need to be taken first in order to act as bases for our aircraft. Our next missions were therefore to gather intelligence about enemy forces on these islands in order for attacks to be mounted by regular forces.

Pretty much as soon as the surrender in Cape Bon had happened a small party of us were flown over to Malta where we overnighted at a submarine depot called Lazaretto near Sliema. We left the next day on submarine called "HMS United". Our objective was to land on the Italian held island of Pantelleria, which was part of the Palagie Islands about 60 miles off the coast of Sicily. This was called Operation Snapdragon. Being deployed by submarine was worse than the conditions on the Arethusa back in Norway; subs were designed for a set number of people not an additional squad from the SAS. I've never forgotten the smell of the diesel engines, the cramped conditions and the sense of our lives being completely in the hands of the Captain and crew.

Pantelleria was a small rocky island, which measured about 8.5 miles by 5.5 miles. It lay in the 'channel' between Tunisia and Sicily and was about 140 miles NW of Malta. Our mission was to land and bring back prisoners for interrogation. In fact when we arrived at the Island the sea was so rough that it was impossible to get ashore so we returned to Malta.

You will recall from the raid on Sark that the moon always played a very important part in our operations, as we needed just enough moon to get ashore and get the job done but with it gone down and complete blackness for us to make our get-away. We waited nearly a month in Malta until the moon was just right for us to try again.

I must admit that as I watched the moon come to the full over Lazaretto submarine base, knowing we were going back a second time, I really wondered if I would ever see another moon like it again. I had a deep sense of foreboding and although I knew these feelings would disappear as soon as we boarded the submarine, as I sat there bathed in moonlight, I wondered if this would be the end of my war. The second time we embarked it was on HMS Unshaken.

I had my quiet moments in the war when I had thought about death and often this happened when there was something I was uneasy about with the upcoming operation. These feelings were only natural and everyone had their moments but it was also important that you didn't dwell on the thoughts, you just had to push them away and get focused otherwise you would end up dead.

This operation has also played heavily on my mind in the years that have passed since the war; I had many years to think about the 'what ifs' and this was one of them. We worked a lot with the Navy and when operating on submarines it was the Captain's tradition, before blokes like us went ashore, to offer us a tot of rum prior to leaving the sub and launching the operation. This seemed completely ridiculous to me so when my turn came I just smiled and said "no thanks". Don't get me wrong, I really enjoyed a drink in the Sergeants' Mess but it just struck me as bloody crackers to be sitting on a submarine swigging rum just before we tactically disembarked and made our way ashore. One of my best mates, whom I served with for a long time, had a laugh about this and 'pulled my leg', he said '"don't worry Stokey if you don't want it I'll have yours." His name was Ernie Herstell, and he was an ex- Hampshire policeman; he was a great bloke.

We left the Sub and the tides and weather conditions were now acceptable for us to get ashore in two inflatable RAF rescue dinghies. We then used our equipment to scale a pretty big cliff and were meant to regroup at the top, with Major Appleyard leading. From here we were going to make our way inland.

Another member of our raiding force, Lt. John Cochrane, writing after the war said :"We had one false start and then began the hardest climb any of us had ever experienced – we pulled ourselves up completely by instinct and every foothold was an insecure one, the rock being volcanic and very porous, crumbling away under our hands and feet. By what seemed to be a miracle, Geoff [Major Appleyard] finally got us safely to the top – covered in scratches – for we had decided to wear shorts so that in an emergency swimming would be easier.

"We were nearly discovered as we reached the top of the cliff which was about a hundred feet high at this point. Geoff and the others were crawling away from the edge towards a path that they could dimly see and I was just pulling myself up over the edge when we heard men approaching. We all froze where we were and then to my horror I felt the edge of the cliff on which I was lying begin to crumble.....

"Just as the patrol came level with Geoffrey, who was lying in the gorse not three feet from their feet, the worst happened. A large stone slipped from beneath me and I waited tensely for the crash as it hit the rocks a hundred feet below me.

"The crash came and Apple and the others prepared to let the patrol have it at short range. But the Italians chattering to each other apparently didn't hear a sound and passed by, little knowing how near to death they had been. We breathed again and prepared to start the work we had been sent to do." [1]

That didn't last long. We hadn't gone a great distance when all hell let loose and what sounded like a heavy machine gun opened fire and each one of us reacted apart from Ernie who was hit and killed. For what seemed like an eternity Major Appleyard and I were involved in one of the most violent firefights of my war with each one of us fighting a fierce battle, killing a significant number of the enemy.

We knew that the operation was compromised and it was really a battle for survival. We had to conduct a

[1] Geoffrey 165/166

fierce fighting withdrawal, leaving Ernie behind on the Island.

We had done all that we could under the circumstances and amazingly, the rest of us we were able to recover back to the submarine. Two hand grenades were dropped into the water as a signal to the submarine, lurking somewhere under the waves, and a short while later she appeared, ready to recover the Team home.

What was remarkable as we made our way through the darkness was that eventually, every other bugger on the island was firing at something but it wasn't us. Most of the island was lit by searchlights and it was clear from the shouts, lights and firing, that the Italians / Germans had thought that it was a full scale parachute landing. We were all so grateful to the Captain of the Unshaken for remaining on station when he had every right to fuck off and leave us. He was a very brave man and against orders risked his crew to save us.

When the adrenalin is pumping and there is a split second to react between life and death you need razor sharp senses. I've had many years to wonder about that night and if I'd taken my tot of rum, instead of Ernie taking both, whether he would have survived. It was also on that night, when we were amongst it, that I heard some of the toughest blokes I'd been to war with, who didn't believe in God or anything else other than the badge we wore and the team we were with, quietly mumbling a prayer to God or anyone other bugger that would listen, whilst involved in some brutal fighting. It remains a mystery to me how many more of us were not left for dead that night. I found out after the war that Ernie's body was never found but he is remembered on the war memorial at Medjez el Bab.

A month later, in June 1943, with a full invasion force preparing to land (Codenamed Operation Corkscrew), Pantelleria surrendered after suffering significant and sustained naval and aerial bombardment. We recovered back to Philippville where we began preparations for our role in the next step to Sicily. It was as well that we couldn't see into the future as Sicily was to be one of the most costly operations the Regiment had ever been involved in and we were to lose many men, and I was to lose many close friends.

SICILY – A FIASCO

The great strength of the Regiment lay in operating in small groups, but this time practically the whole Regiment was to be dropped at various points behind enemy lines in Sicily on different operations; Major Appleyard was the overall drop supervisor. He had been previously injured and couldn't jump. It was early July 1943.

Originally, we had been briefed that about 80 to 100 of us were to be landed on the North coast of Sicily by two specially fitted out submarines sailing from Malta, and we were tasked with making a nuisance of ourselves attacking railways, disrupting communications and ambushing enemy convoys. The idea is that we would remain in Sicily until the main landing had taken place and then join up with our own forces when we were able.

For whatever reason this plan was changed time and again, right up to the last minute. In the end a number of separate 'main' operations were undertaken and the main airborne drop was to be huge. Soldiers get used to people messing around with things and generally adapt to it but this felt different. It was as if it was being made up as we were going along and the main change was that the operation was to switch from sea to air and separate main forces were to be landed in different places.

The change in plan gave everyone a problem as we had neither the equipment nor aircraft (nor for a number of the men the training) to undertake a drop like this. Whilst I was by now an experienced parachutist, many of our new recruits had only basic jump experience. There was also something very different about our operation because the RAF couldn't supply the planes for such a large force (a great number of blokes from different air landing Regiments were being deployed by glider) and so we were being flown and dropped by American C-47 Dakota troop carrying aircraft.

When we had a look around these planes we realised they were absolutely bloody ideal for our kind of work being really well suited to parachute operations. Our only worry, which we expressed to Major Appleyard, was that the American aircrew flying them had absolutely no combat experience and we also knew that they hated night flying. This didn't bode well for our jump into Sicily or for those being launched by glider.

For anyone who doesn't know anything about parachuting, when a group of blokes jump together they usually have to be dropped from a very low height, about 500 feet, and have to exit the aircraft pretty quickly so they spend only seconds in the air and land closely together as a tight knit fighting unit. This requires the aircraft to fly straight and level on the run-in to the dropping zone and of course, it's at this time that the aircraft is most vulnerable to really effective enemy anti-aircraft fire which sometimes could sound and look far worse than it was. You get warnings and cues so you can prepare yourself to jump, such as twenty minutes to go, followed by actions stations, the red light would then go on followed by the green light which meant 'jump'. This allowed you to be ready to exit the aircraft with all of your kit secured.

As we checked our kit and then boarded the aircraft in North Africa, I think all of us knew that this wasn't going to go well. We were meant to land and attack strong points in advance of the main force. The flight to the area of operations was uneventful, but as soon as we started to near the drop zone, in the darkness, our aircraft came under fire and the pilot started to throw the aircraft all over the sky. Of course we ended up in a completely tangled mess and there was no way we could have jumped. As it was, the pilot made his mind up to turn the plane around and we headed back to Africa.

On arrival back at the airstrip, we were very, very angry but it was only later that I was to learn just how costly this had been. We slept fitfully through the day in an olive grove beside the dusty airfield and waited again for night. We knew that some of our mates had been dropped but many of us, the majority, would have to go back a second time the following evening.

Shortly before dark we took off again and on the run-in to the DZ all of us knew we would be dropped anywhere but where we were meant to be. We also knew that two of our planes had been hit and set on fire and one of them had on board Major Appleyard and the other a group of my best mates with whom I'd served since the beginning of the war; they all perished.

The crew informed us that our Dakota was nearing the drop zone and it altered course. Eventually the red light went on and then the green light lit up and we jumped knowing full well that we wouldn't have a fucking clue where we were landing. We were unable to achieve our main objective due to being dropped in the wrong place, but we spent a week or so behind enemy lines ambushing vehicles and patrols, cutting telephone wires - generally creating mayhem and havoc before joining up with the main invading force.

It was only when we eventually arrived back at Philippville that we were to learn how significant our losses had really been. The Navy had picked up a number of bodies of men that had been dropped wrongly into the sea, some of our blokes who were in gliders had also been cast adrift too early and these too were found drifting in the sea. We were absolutely furious and it was as a result of this that we were promised that we would never again be dropped by American planes and aircrew.

As a sequel to this story, about a year later I was in a German prisoner of war camp and met one of my mates, also a Sergeant, who had been officially listed as missing in Sicily. He told me that he had been put down in a glider with an anti-tank gun crew. After a successful landing they were amazed that it was so quiet. The next morning from the copse in which they concealed themselves, they saw a peaceful valley with people working in the fields, the birds were singing and there was absolutely no sign of the war. There was some discussion amongst the crew and they wondered whether an armistice had been signed during the night.

About midday they hitched the anti-tank gun behind the jeep and set off to look for the enemy. He told me that they drove through a tiny village with people waving, this happened at the second village but at the third village a heavy machine gun opened fire and they were caught right in the killing zone. Three of his crew were killed and two badly wounded. He surrendered to the Germans and it was as he was talking to them he discovered that they'd been dropped in bloody Italy instead of Sicily. The drop on Sicily was for me a real low point, loosing half the Regiment, some really great blokes, just because we had been flown by inexperienced pilots.

As a historical note, the airborne drop on Sicily that preceded the main landings was one of the worst self-inflicted disasters of WW2. The joint US / British airborne forces were due to be dropped by parachute, and landed by glider, in advance of the main sea landings on 10th July 1943.

We were meant to be jumping on the very first night in support of the British First Air Landing Brigade. The inexperience and fear of C47 Dakota pilots, which had become so obvious to us prior to the drop, cost hundreds of lives as gliders were cast off miles from their objectives so the Dakota pilots could avoid the anti-aircraft fire; many gliders landed in the sea and for days bodies washed up on the shore. The US paratroopers that were to follow us on subsequent nights fared even worse for different reasons. Hundreds of planes were shot out of the sky by our own forces as they flew at night over the sea convoy transporting assault forces to the beach landings. The sailors feared they were being attacked and once the firing started it didn't stop. Paratroopers jumped randomly to escape the burning planes and as they fell to the ground they were shot by friendly forces who thought they were Germans. The ships gunners and forces ashore were unaware that they were killing their own countrymen.

It was now that I started to reflect on the fact that by the law of averages I wouldn't survive the war and it was after Sicily, as I looked around at the many new strange faces, that I knew in my heart that the next operation was likely to be my last. Anyone who has been in combat for a long time and who says that they don't have these thoughts, is a liar. I've said before that they don't last long, that you can't afford to dwell on them and you have to move on, but as I looked around at Philippville I began to realise I'd probably not survive our next operation. With the fall of Sicily it was obvious that Italy would be the next step on the road to invading Germany. Italy had always been considered the 'soft underbelly' of Hitler's forces and therefore, it came as no surprise when PHP talked to us about Operation Speedwell.

OPERATION SPEEDWELL: ITALY AND ROME

We were briefed on the raid and told we were to take part in an operation to support the invasion of Italy that was imminent, with the raid due to take place between the 3rd – 9th September. Most people will know that Italy is a long thin Country that is shaped like a boot, running North West to South East. Our main allied forces would be attacking the toe and then working their way up through Italy to Austria. The invasion was timed to coincide with a complete surrender of the Italian Forces who had been fighting alongside the Germans. It didn't mean the Italians would start fighting the Germans, it just meant in theory that they wouldn't be fighting us!

Despite this, it was logical that Hitler would rush reinforcements and thousands of troops and armour from northern Europe down into Italy in order to repel our allied invasion, and this is where we came in. The idea was that we would be dropped hundreds of miles behind enemy lines in northern Italy and blow up a number of German military troop / tank trains in tunnels in the Bologna area; this would slow down German reinforcements that we knew would be heading south to bolster Italy against our invasion. To be honest, after the fuck up in Sicily, when we were dropped in significant numbers, this felt more like the kind of thing that we were used to. It was always customary at the end of the briefing to be asked 'any questions' and there was some humour when Lt Anthony Greville-Bell who was about 21, asked how we were to get home and he was told – "that's up to you". In other words, after completing the mission we would be on our own.

On the day of the Op we left Philippville and headed for Kairouan airbase in Tunisia. Sometime later Bebe Daniels and I did a final kit check and everybody seemed pretty relaxed. It was late afternoon on Tuesday 7th September 1943 and we would be dropping as two sticks by Albemarle deep behind enemy lines in the Apennines in northern Italy; the raid was led by PHP who also commanded our stick. Despite the losses in Sicily, I was jumping with some old mates – Tim Robinson (Robbie), Len Curtis, Bebe Daniels and a young Italian speaking Scot from Edinburgh called Pete Tomasso.

We were being dropped by Albemarle which was a really awful aircraft to jump from. PHP should not have been dropped that night as he had badly injured his back when he jumped into Sicily. He had insisted that he go and the Medical Officer had given me tubes of painkiller to spray on his spine which I did well before we jumped; David Stirling knew nothing of his injury and if he had known he would not have let PHP jump.

At about 6.30pm Stirling saw us off, and about 5 hours later, just before midnight, on a moonlit night we were dropped north west of Castiglione, in the mountains north of Spezia. PHP jumped first and I followed, with Robbie jumping after me. Our Drop Zone (DZ) was a small Italian village not far from a lake and the RAF had put us bang on our DZ right on time. I heard PHP's usual shout as he left the aircraft; we were being dropped from about 7000 feet.

For anyone that has done any military parachuting they will say that this sounds quite high for the kind of drop we were doing but the mountains were about 4000 feet high. I could see everybody clearly in the moonlight, but before we landed I was caught by a gust of wind which forced me to swing out of line and PHP yelled 'watch your drift Stokes, watch your drift', and I yelled back 'ok sir'. Everything was so clear, especially the lakes just to the North. PHP half waved his arm and I waved back.

The landing was a bit of a mess to say the least. There was a heavy ground mist and the wind was gusting about 25mph. The bloody wind blew me straight into the side of a chimney and when I hit it I knew I'd really done myself some damage which felt like a rupture. The whole village seemed to wake up and I needed to get out as quickly as possible but I was really tangled so had to drop out of my harness. It's at moments like that when you are dangling there all alone having clattered into a fucking house that you think 'it's not going to end like this, dangling here, shot in my harness'. Needless to say I got a move on but had to leave my chute attached to someone's chimney!

The drill, on hitting the ground, was that we were meant to hide our parachutes, jump jackets and helmets. Naturally, that didn't happen with me. Struggling to get free had taken a bit of time so I should, by then, have seen PHP but as I hadn't heard from him I started moving towards Robbie's position and we actually met half way as he had come to find me. I later learned that nearly everyone had had a difficult landing, Robbie landing on his face and Lt Greville-Bell hitting a tree.

Sadly, that final wave in the air was the last I saw of PHP, although Pete Tomasso had heard him call out. When you are on the ground you have drills for 'rolling up' the stick and after about an hour we had all regrouped apart from PHP. We had also jumped with a couple of containers holding rucksacks, weapons, ammunition and explosives, and recovered these as well. The drill was for number one in the stick (PHP) to move back to number two (me); we would then move to number three (Robbie) and so on until the whole stick was together.

It makes sense to get away from the DZ as quickly as possible but against drills, Robbie and I left the others together and spent over and an hour looking for PHP before it became too dangerous and we had to move on. The three of us had been together for most of the war so neither Robbie nor I had any regrets about spending time trying to find him even though this was against orders. We discovered much later that he had been shot after landing and was later buried in Baigo, Italy. After the war he was reburied in the British Military Cemetery in Florence. I often thought of him after the war and could picture him stark bollock naked, except for a tie, going into the Officers' Mess tent at Philippville.

Lt Greville-Bell was in a really bad way having broken his ribs so we decided to lay up for the night – it was Wednesday 8th September and Philippville felt like a long way away. Whilst I was also in significant pain (I had suffered a bad rupture), I thought it best not to share this with anyone. We distributed Greville-Bell's kit between us and then moved off up a small mountain next to the village, with Greville-Bell being dragged on a parachute. Robbie and I led the way which was pretty hard going as the hillside was covered with large, dense trees. There was no way the operation was going to be executed as planned so we decided to rest for a couple of hours, regroup, and re-plan.

At daybreak we watched from the safety of our laying up point as the village was searched by a good number of Germans. We reorganised into two groups of three; Robbie, me and Len Curtis in one and Lt Greville-Bell, Bebe Daniels and Pete Tomasso in the other. Our target was the Bologna-Prato line, north of Florence. We split what kit we had between the two groups including the plastic explosive, sardines, biscuits and tea. We all moved off together and stayed that way until about mid-day when we said our goodbyes. We had been moving with full kit across difficult terrain at a cracking pace. Robbie, Len and I continued until about two o'clock in the afternoon when we rested under the cover of a thick forest.

We decided it was best to lay-up and move only at night and we reckoned on about 4 nights march, across very rough terrain, to our target. Despite this, we were still keen to put as much distance as possible between us and the DZ, so we set off again at about 7.30pm and as expected it was really tough humping full kit over really harsh low alpine terrain. In addition, we were surviving daily on a handful of raisins, a few biscuits and a bit of cheese. Despite the lack of food it was water that was the problem. We had jumped in with two full water bottles but when you are physically pushing yourself your body needs water more than food, however, we didn't have much of either. The plan was to take more risks after we had executed the mission but it would be completely pointless actively searching out either food or water and getting caught before this.

When you stopped and selected a site for laying up (to rest) it was pitch black and you tried to select somewhere that had good escape routes but was in excellent cover. When we stopped in the early hours of 10th Sep we were in a valley and had great cover and we could hear the sound of a stream not too far away. On waking on the morning of the 10th it allowed us each in turn to get a good wash and shave.

It's hard to explain to people who have never been in this position how such a small act can lift your spirits (even when done in cold water). You had to assess the risks and benefits of doing this but in this case we knew we were completely safe. I even managed a cigarette inside my sleeping bag and it was absolutely fantastic! I can't tell you how this small act made me feel. I was still in a lot of pain but there was no point in telling

Robbie or Len as there was nothing they could do; I figured I was still holding my own and until such time as I started to be a hindrance I should just get on with it.

Over the next few nights we closed in on our objective and I prepared the explosive charges that I was going to use to blow up the train inside the tunnel. By the night of 14th September (having been dropped in the early hours of 8th September) we had arrived in Verino and it was a short distance from here that we were going to carry out the attack. We now had to be extremely cautious but despite this, as we made our way quietly through large back gardens towards the railway line, we came across tomatoes and grapes which we picked and stuffed our faces as we were bloody starving and dehydrated. Bliss.

It was the middle of the night as we crossed the tracks and made our way up a dried up river bed, passing a small manned power house before climbing an embankment to the mouth of the tunnel. It's a good feeling being exactly bang on target and we stopped short and listened ready to deal with any sentry but it wasn't defended at that time. After checking that no trains were approaching I laid the charges, being covered by Robbie and Len. I then moved back to the two of them and the three of us made for the cover of a small wood at the top of a very steep- sided quarry.

We had just made it to the top when we heard the very faint sounds of a train in the distance through the tunnel. Most people won't know that sound seems to travel more in the stillness of the night; noises you might not hear in the day become amplified. It was at this point that I had everything crossed but there was absolutely nothing more I could do. Either everything would work or we would be going back into the tunnel. The noise was growing louder when there was a massive flash that lit up the night followed by an almighty explosion that echoed around the 'closed in' hills and valleys.

I remember so clearly a moment of almost unearthly silence before all hell broke loose and a small fire-fight developed below us. I've no idea who the hell was firing at who but we took this opportunity to move off pretty quickly with the job completed. It never ceased to amaze me but the natural reaction of people who have been attacked was to fire at anything, everything, even if they didn't know what they were firing at. The firefight went on for what felt like ages, which I remember thinking at the time was quite funny, only fading as we got further and further away.

It won't surprise you that we broke nearly every speed marching record ever attempted as we put some distance between us and the target. We really went at it over some fearsome terrain and stopped after about 3-4 hours before first light. Despite laying up and resting through the day we were all still on alert and were aware that this was a dangerous time, consequently we hardly got any rest. We cracked on as soon as we could before midnight, again really pushing it until about 0430am. We were by now surviving on a few biscuits and raisins. On the night of the 15th September we set off at 2300hrs but by now we were all physically very tired, weak, and dehydrated. It was about this time that I started to feel in a lot of pain as the supreme physical exertions had really aggravated my rupture. We didn't make much progress but thankfully I didn't feel this was down to me; it was simply because all of us were completely knackered.

Over the next couple of days in one of our laying-up points we managed a full bath in a covered stream and a mug of tea; job done. I was just about coping and was still managing to hide my injury. I know it's hard for people to imagine but the terrain was so tremendously difficult and despite being supremely fit, tackling this on a hand full of raisins, a few biscuits and a few gulps of water, meant that your body eventually starts to pack-up.

So by the 17th September, ten days after we had dropped, our rations ran out and we decided to start taking far more risks. We began by moving shorter distances, travelling during daylight and we also began buying food. Money is an important commodity behind enemy lines and we had dropped with quite a lot. On about 19th September we managed to buy a loaf of bread, some eggs and cheese. It tasted like a feast fit for kings.

It was whilst we were being so bold that on a track, deep in a wood, we came across two Italian soldiers. As far as we were concerned they were still very much the enemy but it ended peacefully when they told us that Italy had now surrendered and the Italians, who had been supporting the Germans, had laid down their arms. It sort of made sense and we believed them. It appeared they were now hiding from the Germans as well– which made 5 of us! I was not too sure what they made of us, full kit, fucked, weapons and hundreds of miles behind enemy lines but one thing was for sure we were not going to tell them what we had been up to so just said we were escaped POWs, which they didn't believe for a minute.

We occupied an empty cottage and were joined by a number of other Italian soldiers who also appeared to be hiding. They told us that the British had now successfully landed at Salerno and that the Germans were defending a front line from Naples to Bari. Putting this in perspective, this was about 600km south from where we were or about the same distance between London and Glasgow.

They cooked, we relaxed for the first time since we had been dropped, we slept, sorted out our kit, eat well and had a hot shave, and wash. It was at this time that a couple of other Italian soldiers joined us and we learned from them about a devastating attack on a German armoured train convoy deep in the mountains at Verino. Robbie, me and Len just shared a look and that was enough.

I was starting to feel a little better as we were not foot slogging across mountains with all our gear. After a couple of days we learned that German road convoys were using a nearby route. We organised everyone into an ambush party and found a suitable ambush position, set the ambush and waited. The thing about an ambush, when it's not just add hoc like ours was, is that you might wait for a couple of days until the target appears. It's usually based on very sound intelligence and even then the enemy can fail to show up. Needless to say we eventually got fed up of waiting, having seen not a sign of a single German, and we headed back to the cottage. Later that evening we decided it was time to move on and we left; we made it clear the only two Italians who were coming with us were the two who were from their Parachute Regiment as it appeared as though they knew what they were doing.

After some discussion we found out that one of the Italian Paras lived in Naples, which is where the British had formed a front line. He suggested that we might be able to make it nearly as far as Naples, travelling with him, on the train. I recall thinking there was something a little bit ironic about this having just blown up one of the major alpine rail links between northern and southern Italy.

Anyway, we ditched our main weapons having broken them down into the smallest working parts and distributed them far and wide. We buried our Bergens, overalls, and the rest of our stuff and bought civilian clothes, an attaché case and some rations. We packed the rations and small arms into the case and thought fuck it. It had to be better than walking. We bought tickets and headed for Crespino Sul Lamone and at about 6pm on 24th September boarded an Italian train to Faenza. It was a very strange experience but we made it to Faenza and changed trains for Rimini. There were a lot of Germans around at each of the stations but again we made it successfully to Rimini when our luck ran out.

The Germans were checking all travel documents, identity cards and papers. Our Italian Para helped us leave the station via a back exit and we made our way with him to a safe house. In the middle of the night we were roused and told to leave immediately as the Germans were doing house to house searches of all of the houses in the area. We buggered off and made our way north into the countryside but now dressed in civvies and no kit we were pretty exposed and freezing cold.

We managed to get a couple of lifts with farmers going south and made our way along the coast road. The change of plan now required us to head in a south *westerly* direction, making for the Apennine Mountains; the plan was to follow the spine of the mountains south to make contact with our advancing Allied forces who were pushing up from the South. We passed through a number of small vineyards and at each one the locals believed we were escaped POWs and treated us to a glass of wine. Imagine that, alcohol for the first time in weeks – 2 glasses and I felt pissed.

The weather was atrocious and we were completely soaked, so, after a hard slog we stopped in the early evening. We made it to a farm where the farmer greeted us like long lost brothers. That night he gave us a bed; sleeping in a real bed was luxury but the only problem was that we were sharing the room with his two young sons who seemed to spend most of the night staring at us in disbelief.

It was about this time that I started to feel very unwell. The physical exertion had taken its toll on my body and I was in a great deal of pain, so much so that I was unable to hide it from Robbie and Len who now guessed that I was in a bad way. We continued to make our way on foot using mainly roads and by September 28th were heading south near Borgo Pace when we recognised the sound of what could only be a convoy of military trucks. We made it into cover just in time as a good number of German soldiers in about 5 vehicles passed us. I wasn't moving too well by now and we found another farm by the road where the farmer led us to a barn and we rested. After waiting until it was safe, they took us into the farm house and we had a tremendous feast before heading back out to the barn. I told Robbie at this point I didn't think I could go on. All the time I had been getting worse and by now I found it very difficult to move. I had developed really bad boils in my groin which were going sceptic and I had also developed scabies. It was clear to all of us that I was struggling. Despite this, I pressed on for a few more days.

Only after the war did I learn that both separate attacks, ours and Greville Bell's party, had succeeded brilliantly. Trains were buried deep in the mountains, taking days of clearance and the supply of German Armour heading south was held up disrupting their reinforcement plans of Southern Italy where our main forces had landed. Our opposite party, led by Lt Greville-Bell, had foot slogged for 73 days over 300 miles to finally reach friendly forces.

PARTING

It was now early October 1943, having been dropped on 7th September and we all agreed the best thing that we could do was to leave me, which would allow Robbie and Len Curtis to move on. It was the 7th October and I had decided to stay with a farmer and his family near Fabriano - I'll never forget the parting. We had been together for a lot of the war and as Robbie turned to wave from the top of the valley I think both of us thought we would never meet again. That was a hard day.

I stayed with the family for about a week but I knew that I had reached a point that if I didn't get proper medical attention my body was going to give up on me. I was very sick and was buggered if my life was going to end in a farmhouse in Italy. I decided that the only place to get proper medical attention and desperately needed surgery, if I could make it, was the Vatican in Rome. I also figured that anything that took me further South had to be a step in the right direction nearer to our allied forces.

The trouble was going to be getting to Rome. Walking was not an option as I was in tremendous pain with my rupture, septicaemia, suffering from scabies and septic boils. Driving was far too risky with lots of Germans on the road and I would have to steal a car that would be reported very quickly. Therefore, with one final effort I thought I would be able to cycle the 230km which I reckoned would take about 4-5 days. I knew that Rome was my only hope of survival as it had an established POW support network which was probably the only one in Italy. So, I stole a bicycle and set off. That journey took every ounce of my physical and mental strength.

The Rome POW network had been established by an Irish priest called Monseigneur O'Flaherty. In the early war years he had been travelling around Italian POW camps visiting British POWs. There were, of course, already a great many British POWs in Italy having been captured during the earlier North Africa campaign. The priest was really well connected and had established a support network for escaped POWs who needed to be hidden from the Germans. I made it to Rome, but after

4 days I was completely exhausted and as I made my way to the safety of the Vatican City. I knew that if I could convince them I was an escaped POW, they would find a way to get me the medical attention I now desperately needed. I could speak very basic Italian and German and they took me in.

The cycle ride had finished me off and I was by now very, very ill and they soon realised that I wasn't who I said I was and they told me it would be far too risky to keep me in the Vatican and I had to leave. It was clear to them that I needed immediate medical attention so they moved me to a safe house nearby; it was a flat that belonged to a young Yugoslavian medical student who was asked to operate on me and treat me. I have no doubt he saved my life; his name was Dr Mirko Skofic.

Can you imagine to my amazement opening a newspaper back in England in 1949 and seeing his face in a large full-page picture holding the beautiful young international Italian actress called Gina Lollobrigida, Hollywood star of the big screen. I thought I had buried so many memories but seeing his picture haunted me for a number of months. He had just married this very beautiful Italian woman.

My recovery was rapid and as soon as I was up and about I started to venture out into the City. I got an immediate sense of the fear with various rival underground movements, spies and double agents all operating, but the Germans were in full control and clearly exerting their authority. It's worth noting that there were many factions in Rome fighting each other and only a few fighting the Germans. Despite the fact that Italy had surrendered, the Germans had rushed into Rome and now held it in an iron-like grip. They were supported by several local Italian fascist groups who believed Italy had made a mistake to surrender and these groups continued to work with the Germans; they were bloody dangerous.

At the other end of the spectrum was the clandestine Communist Party who were trying to organise some form of resistance through the formation of patriotic action groups. Despite it being against orders, I knew I could be of most use assisting and organising these action groups, so I spent several months living in

Rome, dodging the Germans and helping the groups organise their resistance and training their people. I knew it would be only a matter of time before the Allies arrived in Rome and so it seemed to make sense to stay and make life as difficult as possible for the Germans.

Back in North Africa many of us had discussed just this kind of situation and it was accepted, as part of our ethos, that we would work with guerrillas and underground movements if it was the only way to continue to 'do our bit'. With my training in explosives, small arms and unarmed combat I was able to be quite effective. The kind of operations that we organised were attacks on installations or German columns such as the one carried out against an SS column marching through Rome. The SS had a fierce and brutal reputation.

You never quite knew how things were going to turn out and there were a number of moments when I thought my number was up. On one truly bizarre occasion I was stopped by the Gestapo but was assisted in escaping by a 17-year-old Italian communist party worker with a wooden leg who knew a way out down the tiny back alleys.

The other ridiculous moment was when I was captured by group of Italians who all belonged to an ultra-fascist group who fully supported the German occupation; they stuck a gun to my head and were about to shoot me but I managed to convince them I was an undercover German! I couldn't help but laugh about both of these surreal events. Despite it being dangerous I could still manage to move about openly, get my hair cut and occasionally, I even got my hands on an English book, English biscuits, and sometimes English cigarettes. Mostly I managed to get hold of this stuff via the Swiss Legation, which remained neutral throughout the war; they thought I was an escaped POW in hiding so offered me, and others like me, help and assistance. It's a good job they didn't know I was helping to organise the resistance and ambushing German convoys.

Then one day, in late March 1944, shortly after an attack on the Germans, I was on a pre-arranged visit to Swiss Legation, when the building was surrounded and despite a struggle, I was captured trying to escape.

Only after the war did I discover from the Americans that I had probably been betrayed by Italian staff from the Vatican who lived in fear of SS reprisals. I never found out if this was true or not. Also, whilst I didn't know it then, it was only two months later that Rome was to be liberated and I would have been back to the SAS.

CAPTURED IN ROME

There were some simple rules about being captured. Doing the job we had done it was something we had always considered and trained for. I had had many days in Rome to think about what I would do if this happened and I knew the first thing I had to do was to convince them that I was an escaped POW who had been in hiding. If they found out who I really was I knew I would be shot.

I had a story about who I was, which unit I belonged to (the Royal Artillery), and that I had been taken POW in North Africa. All of this was simple, close to the truth and believable. Secondly, if you were going to think about escaping it needed to be pretty soon after capture because once you were in the machine, and being moved further back to Germany, things would start to get more and more difficult.

Each one of us knew we had a duty to escape. There were a number of reasons for this: firstly, it would tie up a good number of German soldiers looking for you;

second your destiny was in your own hands; thirdly, it was always possible to bump into partisans or guerrillas and help them organise local resistance (like I had done in Rome); and finally there was always the remote possibility that you could make it back to your own front lines!

Despite all of this, my first task was to convince them I was a POW in hiding. It was clear to me that I had been' turned in', someone had told them who I was and where I would be, and the soldiers who seized me were Gestapo officers and troops. I was taken immediately to Gestapo HQ in central Rome and my interrogation began. You had to keep it simple and I had a story and my best chance of survival was to stick to it no matter how tough it got.

There are only two periods of the war I still find it difficult to think about and these are times I would not want to share. One of them was now, in the week after my capture. The second was to come later after I had escaped for a third time and had been taken to a very small punishment barracks in Bad Tolz, Germany. The memories of these two difficult periods of my life are too painful for reflection so can't be shared.

Suffice to say that after spending a very bad week at the hands of the Gestapo they finally believed my story that I had escaped from a POW camp and was on the run, and had sought refuge in Rome. So far, so good. I knew that things would now get much easier very quickly. The Gestapo had me removed to a small transit camp south of Rome where there were only a few people, mainly Brits, some of whom had been captured the night before and moved north to Rome.

I don't think my fellow POWs knew quite what to make of me with my clean haircut, civilian clothes and grasp of Italian and German, covered in cuts and bruises. I had to repeat my story all over again about being an escaped POW as I wasn't taking any chances. We were pretty closely guarded at this stage and I just accepted what would happen, would happen. It was important that no one, not even fellow POWs, knew my background. It was far better to be low key and anonymous.

We were then moved, always at night, through a series of transit camps up into a camp at a place called Bolzano. They moved us at night so the trains wouldn't be attacked by our own Allied Air Forces who would have had no idea from the air that we weren't a German troop-carrying train. It was whilst in the first transit camp I made my first escape attempt but it was disaster as I was recaptured after 24 hours having been reported by a group of Fascists.

In the third camp I tried again but this was even less successful and after 3 days I was reported by a local German sympathiser and was discovered pretty quickly. By now they were getting a bit fed-up with me and they let me know it. As a result of this by the time I reached Bolzano I was in no fit state to do anything; I was starving, as thin as an X-ray film and covered with lice, lumps, bumps, and bruises. It was here in Bolzano that a couple of us were singled out for special treatment. There were hundreds, it actually felt like thousands, of people being transported by railway wagon; we escapees were packed so tightly you couldn't sit down.

The door was closed and we knew it was next stop Munich. That journey over 3 days will stay with me for ever; the stench, the horror, and the filth. Also, we were now being moved by day and not by night. Seeing how men reacted to those conditions was heart breaking in a way and it took every ounce of my self-belief and training to hold on to my sense of sanity during that journey. On the second day our train was attacked by Allied aircraft (who wouldn't have known it was filled with POWs) and several people in my carriage were killed; they died standing up and there was nothing we could do to stop them dying as we were so tightly packed.

The randomness of that act, those who died and those who didn't, reminded me of all my friends who had been lost including PHP, Ernie Herstell and Major Appleyard. I hated that journey – it truly broke several men. You can tell from a man's eyes when they have lost every ounce of self-discipline and belief and I felt sorry for those on that journey who hadn't been trained the way we had, being able to draw on a deep reserve of inner strength.

The journey finally ended in Munich where we were transferred to a proper POW camp. It was about July 1944, 11 months after we had jumped into Italy and about two months after I had been captured in Rome. The camp was organised and well run, and compared to the journey, the conditions were pretty good. After a few days I had regained some of my strength and 'played the game' in order to get a transfer to one of the work camp detachments in the suburbs of Munich; POWs were deployed to repair the massive bomb damage that had been inflicted on the City during the 1000 bomber raids. I knew if I could get the transfer it would allow me another attempt at escape. This time, however, I knew breaking out deep inside Germany was going to present a great many more challenges than escaping in Italy.

I was in Munich on the nights of the 1000 bomber raids and it was like nothing I had ever experienced and nor have I ever since. The bombing never ceased, it was relentless. One night hundreds of aircraft attacked the City with incendiary bombs; they were over the City in an hour and then gone. The camp we were in was hit and I really thought during that hour that that was how my war was going to end, blown up by our own allied aircraft. I saw a bomber crash land no more than 500 yards away from where I was standing. It just hit the ground and exploded, bursting into a massive ball of flame. I remember thinking what a terrible end for the very brave crew.

It had been a still, calm and chilly night before the bombers came but they created a fire storm that destroyed the City. The fire was so intense and fierce that it created wind like a tornado, sucking all of the air into it. It was difficult to breathe and hard to stand. I had never seen war delivered in this way and a small part of me felt very sorry for the civilians, such as old people, women and children who were caught up in all of this; the devastation was truly terrible.

ESCAPE FROM MUNICH

Despite the devastation in Munich, the bombing raid gave me the opening I needed for my third escape attempt. I asked for a transfer to one of the smaller camps where work parties were being used to fill the craters and bomb damage. Most of the buildings were left shattered with walls and roofs destroyed. People tried to go about their business but nothing felt normal with cars passing between huge piles of debris that had been cleared out of the way. We would get 'patted down' regularly to make sure we not trying to smuggle tools or weapons back into camp.

Over the next few days of going back to the same area I sensed that the moment was right to try for my third attempt. We had some new sentries assigned to our work party and I thought it would take them a while to get to know our faces. So one lunchtime I stole some civilian clothes and planted them amongst the rubble. I had also noticed that several pushbikes were leant up against the same wall every day. The following morning whilst the sentry was distracted I grabbed the

157

bundle, changed into the civilian clothes, walked across to the pushbike and got on it and rode away. Nothing dramatic or brave about it, I just peddled away while no one was looking.

My plan was to head south towards the Brenner Pass and Italy, taking me closer to our own advancing troops. I also knew that if I could make it into Italy, the locals were more likely to be sympathetic and I'd get food and shelter; besides this I knew how things operated in Italy and was very familiar with the geography. I couldn't help but think about my last journey on a bloody pushbike behind enemy lines and thankfully I felt in much better shape than when I had cycled to Rome.

Using back roads I cycled out of Munich and then dumped the bike, heading for the mountains. I knew the terrain between Munich and the Brenner Pass would be rugged and demanding. Munich is the Capital of Bavaria, and the countryside consisted of very tough farming mountain folk who would either shoot me or report me, or probably both. So I made my way on foot, travelling always at night and laying-up during the day, across the foothills of the Alps which run towards the German / Austrian border. There was plenty of water and food that I could obtain through foraging so I wasn't going to starve. Despite being fit again, I was extremely undernourished, and the going was therefore very slow, although this was a good thing as I needed to be very cautious without a map, compass or a weapon.

I had managed to cover about 60 miles over 4 nights and had made it just south of a small town called Bad Tolz, which was about 15 miles north of the Austrian border. I saw the town as an obstacle and knew I would need to go around it and had selected my laying-up point for the night to the South, well away from the town in the surrounding hills.

I concealed myself deep in the woods before first light and covered myself with bracken and undergrowth. I needed to sleep and knew that concealment was my best and only protection, and I wouldn't move again until it was completely dark. No matter what people might tell you, even when you are deep behind enemy lines, you have to sleep. You don't need to sleep for long but sleep is critical if you are not going to make mistakes.

About an hour after bedding down I was woken from a deep sleep in complete shock being kicked awake by several live armed SS officer cadets and their instructors who had literally just stumbled onto my position. After a brief struggle I was hit with a rifle and had a pistol held to my head. As I took in the scene I couldn't fucking believe it; I was in the middle of what felt like a wood clearance exercise. It was clear the game was up and I was taken prisoner (again) by the SS. Unfortunately for me, I didn't know that Bad Tolz was the home of one of the largest SS Officer Training Camps in Germany.

It won't surprise you that we were well trained in recognising uniforms, weapons and vehicles because reconnaissance and reporting had been a critical part of our role. I knew, therefore, what I was in for at the hands of these fanatical bastards. The SS were hard, ruthless, extremely loyal and exceptionally well trained. I couldn't believe my bad luck. My experience at the hands of the Gestapo in Rome had been no picnic so I sort of knew what was to come. My only saving grace was that I was now a proper escaped POW and wouldn't have to bullshit about that. There could be absolutely no connection between me and the blowing up of the trains and tunnels in Italy. Despite this, they must have known I was no ordinary soldier.

I was pretty badly beaten and then thrown on a truck and transported back to a major barracks complex, only then realising it had been like sticking my head in a hornet's nest. I really expected to be shot immediately but to my surprise and relief I was thrown in a tiny cell. I spent a very uncomfortable week in a very small SS punishment barracks and was interrogated every day. After a week, suddenly, I was informed I was to be transported to a very large and well organised POW camp called Stalag VIIA. This was an enormous relief to me as I knew my chances of survival had just improved dramatically. As far as they were concerned I was an escaped POW from Munich and was Sergeant Horace Stokes of the Royal Artillery – not the SAS!

STALAG VIIA – MOOSBURG

Stalag VII A had been established as a POW camp shortly after the beginning of the War in September of 1939. It was called Kriegsgefangenen - Mannschafts - Stammlager (Stalag) VIIA and was situated just north of Moosburg not too far from where I had been captured at Bad Tolz. The camp had been built originally to house Polish prisoners taken after the early German offensive against Poland in 1939. The camp was absolutely vast with a mix of British, Americans, Russian, Polish and Canadian troops.

The perimeter of the camp, as far as I could see, was a regular pattern of guard towers each with a heavy machine gun. These military parapets were well constructed and well sighted, and they covered the entire perimeter. Between the towers were impassable barbed wire barriers, that were also covered by effective fire; these were very well lit at night. The sharp, spiked wire was also used to create two 12-foot high walls separated by more coiled barbed wire. Inside the camp there were rows and rows of drab, unpainted, squat buildings. It was very cold, and bleak, and the surrounding area was heavily wooded. However, compared to where I had just come from it felt like heaven.

It took me some time to fully recover from my recapture and treatment but I quickly found my way around and the camp was truly enormous.

On arrival, once you had registered and had all of your details taken, you were issued with POW identity discs and a POW number, mine was 129850. Despite it being very well organised, it was obvious that a number of people had completely 'let themselves go' or as we used to say they had 'gone native'. They were bedraggled, unkempt, unwashed and mentally they had given up – broken men. Yes, it was pretty unpleasant but despite the dysentery, diarrhoea and fleas, whatever the conditions, you had to remain focused, and retain your self-discipline trying to stay clean, smart and fit.

Our rations were meagre and we had things such as tea or coffee for breakfast, with bread if we were lucky, soup for lunch made from cabbage or vegetables, and for dinner, boiled potatoes with a piece of cheese or very occasionally a slice of sausage. Sometimes, more often than not in fact, there was no food at all. But life could have been a damn sight worse – by the law of averages I should have been killed on so many previous occasions.

You could always tell new arrivals as they had their heads shaved and had been de-loused in great tubs that doubled as baths. Some POWs had been forced to walk hundreds of miles to get to the camp, many of them were in a truly dreadful state. People had marched for months from as far away as Poland. Their stories were very horrifying and they told us that anyone 'falling out' on the march, that is they had not managed to keep up or had collapsed, had been shot dead and their body left beside the road. What a terrible way to die.

The bunks we slept in were wooden slatted and the mattresses filled with straw and ridden with fleas – it sort of reminded me of my days as a child at home! Mostly, people slept on the floor as there was just no room with hundreds of people occupying a small hall meant for far fewer numbers. The camp housed over

100,000 allied POWs by the end of the war. At night you were locked in and they let attack dogs roam free in the compound with strong searchlights covering the ground from the high watch towers that housed the heavy calibre machine guns. The rows of high fences topped with barbed wire made sure we weren't going anywhere. Despite this, my recollection of the guards was that they treated us well and were, in the main, fair.

New prisoners were arriving and leaving all the time so we were getting information. It was clear our Allied Forces were making very good progress with the Americans pushing hard to occupy our area of south Germany and Bavaria, and particularly the bridges over the Rivers Amper and Isar.

In April 1945, about a year after I had been captured in Rome, the US 14th Armoured Division pushed south and after some fierce fighting arrived just short of Moosburg. Apparently the American Forces were unaware that the largest POW Camp in Germany was situated just a few miles away from their position. As the US Forces advanced they met brief but heavy resistance from SS units who were retreating and had, by chance, also stopped at Moosburg.

The fighting intensified around us and we could hear the sound of heavy weapons, tanks, mortars and machine guns which were very close. We woke one morning and most of the Germans had left, slipping away quietly in the night; this meant the end must be near. We replaced the guards with our own, which did feel strange, but we thought that liberation was imminent but it didn't come.

Replacing the guards may seem odd but the last thing anyone needed in the middle of a battle raging around us was tens of thousands of POWs spilling out into the countryside. The theory was the safest place for everyone would be inside the Camp. If this didn't happen it was inevitable that some POWs would rape and plunder their way through local German villages seeking reprisals, or get caught up in the fighting.

Keeping people in, however, was increasingly difficult to achieve. The reason was that shortly after New Year 1945 the conditions inside had become really shocking with no sanitation, very little food and lots of disease. When the Camp wasn't liberated quickly it changed everything for me as I could see any liberating Army keeping us cooped up for quite a while. This changed things and I now wanted to be outside as quickly as possible. Over about a week in April things went from bad to worse as absolutely nothing was coming into the camp; food was unobtainable and human excrement was everywhere. Men acted like savages as conditions deteriorated daily. It was ironic but it was of course far worse than when the Camp had been run and organised by the Germans. Each day we were told that the Americans were laying a road to liberate the Camp and each day things got worse.

During my time in the camp I had got to know an American soldier and we became particularly good friends; he was called Lester Koch and was from Long Island, New York. If I'm honest, I generally despised the Americans in captivity as they were the worst at letting themselves go but Lester was a sound trooper and had a bit of our bulldog spirit . It was obvious the place was now turning into a fucking nightmare so four of us, two Brits and two Yanks, managed to get some wire cutters and in the night made our way out of the camp and towards the town of Moosberg.

As it happened, on 29th April 1945 the most senior British and American Officers finally managed to join up with the Red Cross and visited the US Force Headquarters so that they could make the Americans aware of the presence of the thousands of allied troops located in the Camp. On 30th April the Camp was liberated.

Of course we were already out and heading for home. Shortly before we reached Moosburg we found an abandoned German Army staff car, stole some white paint and wrote all over it "POWs heading for Channel Ports" then set out onto the local German roads. Our plan was for us Brits to drive through the US Sectors and the Americans to drive through the British Sectors. In this way we thought we would manage to gain some sympathy, food and petrol! We drove for a few days passing through various US checkpoints and they showered us with cigarettes called Camels and Lucky Strikes that tasted bloody fantastic. We had fresh fruit, tins of meat and all sorts of other things. It felt like I was in Heaven.

We had also decided that we would get petrol wherever we could so whenever we got to about a quarter of a tank, if we found a refuelling point we would stop and fill up. At one point we came to a long convoy of trucks queued to refuel and so we joined the back of the queue. We had been stopped for a while when an American Military Police jeep with a high ranking officer passed alongside us and stopped. He got out and spoke to us and then ordered our vehicle out of line and told us to follow him. We drove to the outskirts of a small town, turned a corner and saw a field full of burned out vehicles. We got out and he gave us a can of fuel and made us set light to the car.

We were all told to report to an American unit based in the historic German town of Ulm that was shattered and completely devastated. It was May 1945 and the Yanks made such a fuss of us. We were de-loused, given fresh clean clothes and lashings of such fantastic food. The weather in southern Germany was absolutely beautiful.

I swam every day in the Danube and my fitness and strength returned.

It must have been a terrible time for my family because back in England the British Press and the BBC were now reporting that all British POWs who were alive had been returned home. To be honest people worrying about me for a little longer was the last thing I was worried about; I was completely happy and just glad to be alive. My family had spent 6 years not knowing where I was or what I was doing so another few weeks wasn't going to make any difference.

Eventually one of the senior American officers, who was from the unit we were attached to, said the arrangement had to end. A few weeks later we were told a staff car was arriving to take us to a local airfield where a Lancaster bomber would be waiting to take us home. And so it did.

<u>HOME</u>

HOME. I was going home! On the flight I couldn't quite comprehend it. Home to my mum and dad, brothers and sisters, my mates and a pint in the local pub. Home to a proper bed, in a proper house. I had slept in tents, in the open under the stars, in the freezing undergrowth, in bombed out buildings and on boats, trains, planes and submarines, and now home to a proper bed. On arriving home I was immediately given three months leave.

And there I was back in Birmingham; I'd left aged 18 and not been home since. It felt surreal with everyone wanting to celebrate my return and the fact that the war had ended but how was it possible for me to share what I'd seen and done with anyone who had not been in the same position. This is a combat soldier's dilemma; I had killed a great number of people, many of them in very close combat; I'd witnessed things that in an ordinary life no human being should witness. I was like many other returning combat veterans who felt torn between elation, deep sadness for fallen comrades, and regret, all wrapped up in a sense of immense pride. I forced myself to reflect that I'd been privileged to be part of some very special units doing things that made a strategic difference.

After my 3 months leave I learned that the 2nd SAS, with whom I'd served most of my war, was to be disbanded. I think most of my Unit had somehow ended up in Norway. I reported to a main army depot in civilian clothes as all my kit had been left in Africa. I was immediately forced into the 'sausage' machine being processed by new peacetime army instructors who, because my records stated Royal Artillery, thought I needed to do some very basic training to learn how to handle and fire a weapon and read a map. It won't surprise you that I didn't take too kindly to this idea and I explained to them why; once we had reached an agreement I was pretty much left alone.

I was then moved quickly to a coastal battery position of heavy guns at Fort Tregantle in Cornwall. To be honest I wouldn't have known the first thing about being a battery sergeant major but because I was badged Royal Artillery that's where I went. Sometimes fate, or luck, plays a part in our destiny and as it turned out, I was so glad that I ended up at Fort Tregantle as it was here that my love affair with Cornwall, that was to last a lifetime, began. By now I had also obtained a full set of uniforms again.

When I arrived in Cornwall the vast majority of senior officers and NCOs took one look at me with my SAS shoulder flashes and parachute wings on my chest, denoting I had served behind enemy lines, and they really didn't know what to do with me. However, after chatting to the commanding officer, it was agreed that I would, pretty much, be left to my own devices. I used to run for miles along the cliffs and swam every day so far out to sea that Fort Tregantle became a tiny spec on the coastline. I was very glad for this time as it allowed me to think, reflect, and normalise.

And then one day I was asked to take a troop of men to set up a centre in Taunton to start processing people out of the Army, it was called a 'demob', or demobilisation, centre. The centre was open 24 hours a day, 7 days a week. Troops would arrive from all over the world. They would be fed, showered, given a medical, issued with ration books, choose shoes, a suit, tie, hat and coat and would then be presented with a railway warrant and taken to the station. All of this was done in 24 hours. I then moved around to different centres until finally in early April 1946, I was asked to report to Manchester demob centre and on 24th April I became a civilian and headed home. It was a year after breaking out of Stalag VIIA and two years after my capture in Rome. I was 25 years old and had seen and done more in my short life than most people could ever imagine.

For one last time I forced myself to think of the faces with whom I'd served on 12 Commando, the Small Scale Raiding Force and the 2nd SAS. I had lost so many good friends and true comrades including Philip Pinckney, Major Appleyard (Distinguished Service Order, Military Cross and bar), and Ernie Herstell – the list could go on and on. Nobody in the Regiment knew what had become of me; my story had never been told in a post operation report because nobody knew that I had survived or what happened to me after Robbie and I had parted at the farmhouse in Italy. I wrote to Robbie to let him know I was still alive.

During my three months post POW leave, and whilst in Cornwall, I had already decided to shut the book on this chapter of my life, vowing never to speak of it again. What was done, was done and I needed to begin a brand new life. This was no different from the millions of other servicemen all over the world who were having to do the same. I also vowed that on 11th hour, on the 11th day of the 11th month for every year thereafter I would quietly remember them in my own way, my comrades, the fallen. I didn't know it at the time but it was actually to be on most nights throughout the rest of my life that I would sit and reflect, in the wee small hours with a small glass of whiskey, about why it was me who had survived, whilst some of my very best friends had been killed. But for now it was time to pick up the pieces and begin again.

POST WAR

It's hard to pack your life into a box and put everything behind you, but that's what I did. Returning home to Birmingham properly this time allowed me to take in the devastation and damage that had been caused by heavy bombing and incendiary raids. Birmingham's industrial heartland had been really badly hit as it had been targeted due to producing guns and aircraft. The City centre was also very badly damaged. I couldn't help but think of that night in Munich when the City had been destroyed and how it must have felt for friends and family here at home when the German bombers came.

There was no work, no fuel, no food, and a sense of desperation. Even the pubs had to open on a rota basis because there was not enough beer and bread was rationed for the very first time. The whole nation had to re-gear from producing war materials and go back to peacetime production. This is what victory looked like.

I was given a final two months paid leave and I knew immediately that I needed to spend it with my brother Johnnie, who was now living and running a business in Sidmouth, Devon. John had been demobbed well before me and had started a business called ACME Household Services. All around the Sid Valley there were a great number of huge grand old houses where vast numbers of rooms had been shut for the whole war due to the lack of servants to maintain the households. John had employed a number of ex-servicemen to renovate the houses and then maintain them, sometimes just going in for a few hours per week. It appeared he was making a real success of it. I had a fantastic working holiday and very much appreciated spending the time with my favourite brother.

Whilst in Sidmouth I had spoken to John about what I was to do and it was obvious I needed to draw on the skills I had had before the war. I spent the money the Army had given me on a small van and drove it back to Birmingham and started a mobile greengrocery round. The business flourished as I drew on all my old contacts in the wholesale market where I'd worked before the war. To be honest it was through my contacts that I managed to do so well.

I was able to get the things people wanted but hadn't been able to get throughout the war years. I was soon supplying Cape fruit including oranges and bananas; indeed, pretty much anything people wanted I was able to get which meant my customer base flourished! Life was good.

Then, as often happens, my world was turned on its head. There is a poem about two paths that diverge in a wood and I should have known that I would take the path less travelled. You see, through the business, I met and fell head over heels in love with a beautiful young woman who had a small son, Graham. I was to learn there was only one problem – she was married and living a very unhappy life. These were the days when women didn't get divorced and marriage was for life - but I was hopelessly in love.

She left her husband, I sold my business, and within days moved back to Sidmouth with both her and her son and we found a very large, furnished, detached house, and opened it as a guest house taking in paying customers – the house was called Glen View. These were heady, happy days. I swam every day from May to October, sometimes so far out to sea that the town would be a tiny dot framed by the valley. I got to know every inch of every walk and there were many days when I found a spot and waited, motionless in deep thick woods, watching the deer go by.

It was also at this time that we had an addition to our family and our baby daughter, Patricia, was born. As often happens, a line between life and death is sometimes joined and our joy at her entering the world was coupled with sadness at the death of my father. He had been very unwell for a number of months, with chronic bronchitis, and both he and my mum had moved from Birmingham to Sidmouth to live with us. They had been with us for about a year when he died. I had hoped that the fresh, clean sea air would have made him feel better but his lungs were far too weak and infected to make any difference.

My brother John and I sat in his room the night he died and spent the whole evening reminiscing about our childhood days back in Small Heath and we laughed when we remembered the old pawnshop and how angry he had been about his suit. As the first light of dawn began to appear his life just ebbed away. Whilst this event cast a small shadow, it was in no way the single catalyst for what was to follow.

The business was in trouble; it may have been over the course of the year we had taken our 'eye off the ball' and we charged too little and fed people too well. In order to try and rectify this I started a 24 hour laundry business servicing the hotel trade but after a short while it failed dismally. It was obvious that something had to change drastically and we took the decision to move back to Birmingham.

We had been in Sidmouth for four and a half years, and in October went back to set up home (for all four of us) in the front room of my mother-in-law's house in Acocks Green in Birmingham. Thankfully, it was a great big Victorian house and somehow we managed to find our own space. I think what made it tolerable was that I got on so well with her family. But the question was – what now? No money, a family and no prospects. I've never been one for self-pity and my time in the SAS had taught me that if you didn't make things happen for yourself then no other bugger was going to make them happen for you.

So, I took a job as a full-time bar cellar man in a city centre pub in the middle of Birmingham. I worked hard and one day a manager from the brewery came to see me and asked if I would be prepared to take on a short–term 'special' assignment. It transpired that the Earl of Harwood and his party had taken over the Bell Hotel in Tewkesbury and they wanted me to go and help manage the place whilst his party stayed there. I don't mind admitting that I was a bit of a socialist and on one level it really made my blood boil. However, on another level it was a work opportunity that was too good to miss. I suppose I knew it would end in tears and on New Year's Day 1952, things erupted and I walked out of the job.

It was about now that my life pretty much reached rock bottom, as I drifted through a series of jobs including a vacuum cleaner salesman, a petrol pump attendant, a printing press salesman and a labourer on a building site. I finally ended up working permanent nights in a factory. It seemed that life had gone full circle from my childhood days in our two bed terraced house in Victoria Road; my family was now so poor that I felt ashamed. In the middle of a long, cold dark night, I lay in bed tossing and turning, and my wife, Joan, woke up and asked quietly 'what's the matter luv'? I said 'I don't know, how can our lives have come to this? I just can't seem to settle down like other men, I can't keep a job and this is no way to live our lives'.

She held me tightly and said 'you are not like other men; something will come up and life will get better, I trust you and love you and know that what is happening now is just a blip. What's most important is that you wake up in the morning and want to go to work and come home happy to us. Just leave the bloody job in the factory'. And the next day I did.

Not long after, I applied for and got a job managing a greengrocer's shop in Mosley, Birmingham. It had a lovely flat above the shop which became our home. I loved the work as it took me back to my roots. Up very early, off to the market where I knew all the old faces and then back to the hustle and bustle of a very large shop. About 6-months later, completely out of the blue, I received a letter from one of the largest brewing and pub owning business in the Midlands, Mitchells and Butlers (M&B). To be honest I had completely forgotten that when I was at my lowest ebb I had written to them and asked to be considered for pub management. I thought at the time that given my experience of running a business and having worked in the licenced trade, I might be in with a shout. So after many months, and when we were settled and I'd forgotten about it, they wrote to me offering me the chance to run my own pub in Aston, close to Villa Park Football Ground. It was called the Red Lion.

Joan and I discussed it and knew it was the right decision to move. We spent a very happy 3 years there and made some truly wonderful friends who were to remain close pals for the rest of my life. We were then offered a very big pubic house in Erdington, Birmingham, called the Norton Inn, right next door to Fort Dunlop.

During my time with M&B I took up the cause of all licensees in Birmingham and was elected chair of the licensees' union. We were never a militant union and for many years, I like to think I brought pragmatism and quiet but firm diplomacy to negotiations on terms and conditions over a period of immense change in the industry. I met managing directors, company shareholders and would like to hope that in a small way, I worked hard for the things that mattered. I always knew I'd done the right thing; we had stability, enough money, a lovely home, and a good life.

Despite this, there was one moment when I considered giving up our life and moving on and that was when, like a bolt out of the blue, I received a letter from my old CO in the SAS, Bill Stirling, who had moved to Rhodesia, South Africa. It was clear after corresponding and doing a little research that this was a real opportunity for a new life and I was really excited about seizing the chance. I knew some of the folk who were out there with him and it struck me as being a land of hard work and opportunity.

Things came to a head, however, when I found my small items of SAS war memorabilia on fire in a metal dustbin in our back garden and my wife with the matches and paraffin! It was clear if I was going, I was going on my own! No choice really when it was put like that and I wrote and thanked him for the opportunity but said we had decided to remain in England.

Despite the years that passed some things, both skills and memories, never seemed to fade. I recall vividly, around the time of my 50th birthday, giving a barmaid the sack for fiddling the till and pocketing money. Two nights later after locking up the pub and cashing up, the doorbell rang at nearly midnight. I opened the door and a youngish bloke about 27 years old stood there. I asked him what he wanted and he asked if I was 'Mr Stokes the gaffer'. I said 'yes' whereupon he produced a bloody big knife and lunged at me; it was the boyfriend of the girl I had sacked.

I don't suppose he expected an old bugger like me to be able to disarm him and hold him until the police arrived but thankfully these kind of things were few and far between. On the whole, it was a wonderful life and I watched my kids grow up and we remained at the Norton until I retired in about 1984. It was only during those last 10 years before retiring that I decided to start work on my personal journal. Yes, it stirred some memories but as my wife would attest to, there hadn't been a single night when I'd not sat for a few minutes and remembered some of the finest blokes in the world. Their faces, laughter, comradeship and pain had remained with me since 1945.

LAST POST

It was a Friday night in early December 1986. There had been a harsh, biting wind blowing across Catterick Moor all day. I had spent most of it on the training area with a troop of new recruits and my instructors. I was serving as one of the officers on Basic Recruit Training Squadron, having arrived at the RAF Regiment Depot via the Platoon Commanders Battle Course at Warminster.

I had called into the Officers' Mess for a quick beer before going on to a friend's house where we were having a pre-Christmas Draw party. I was dressed in bow tie and dinner suit and looking forward to a really great evening. One of my pals shouted across the bar "Stokesy, phone call at reception for you". I headed out to reception and lifted the receiver.

It was my sister, Pat, she was crying and could hardly get her words out; "Pete, I don't know how to say this but Dad's dying, he has only a few weeks to live and he wants you to come home, can you come as soon as possible, please". I have often heard people say that there are moments when the world stops, when you can hear and see life going on around you but it's as though you are frozen in time. That's how I felt.

When you are not on operations, the Armed Forces are superb at moving quickly to allow you to be near a loved one when they are dying. I spoke to my commanding officer and the following day, Saturday, I made my way back to Birmingham to my parent's house in the Lickey Hills. They lived in a small house in a close-knit community of ex publicans (you will recall that my dad had run a public house called the Norton in Erdington, Birmingham for over 30 years). That long drive home was so painful. When I arrived home my mum, my sister and my auntie met me and we all hugged and cried. My dad was lying in bed and I went in to greet him; he looked very frail and I sat down and held his hand. I then hugged him, and I cried again.

After a while he lifted my chin and looked at me and said "my son, life is going to be difficult for the next few weeks. The family is going to fall apart, your mum and your uncles and aunties are all going to need your support. You are going to need to be strong for them and for me. There are people I want to see and things I want to say to you before I die, so from this moment forward I want to see you with a loving smile on your face every time we sit together"; and so that's what I did.

My Dad explained to me that he had decided that he wanted to spend his last few days with friends and family, re-living some of the happiest parts of his life. He told me that he wanted to spend Christmas Day as a family, at my brother's house, with everyone around him. He said that after he had done this he would die a happy man.

Over the next few days friends came and went, I would meet them and we would hug, I would tell them that dad wanted them to be strong and not to be upset but to speak with him and reminisce and be happy, and share their memories. I knew that he could manage about 45 minutes to an hour with each person before it was time for me to open the door and let them know it was time to leave. They would embrace and I would escort them to the door and only once outside would they breakdown and cry, and over the days that passed this would happen again and again.

It was at this time that my Dad gave me his treasured journal and he asked me to read it, which of course I did. It was in those pages that I learnt some of the remarkable things that he had done and some of the terrible things he had witnessed in a few short years when he changed from a boy to man. We talked for ages about his journal. I think that having seen me graduate as a young platoon commander and listening to me moan about arduous training in the Brecon Beacons for one patrol competition or another, he knew that in some small way I could relate to, and understand, the story he wanted to tell.

With each passing day he became a little weaker but when I looked into his eyes that steel and strength was still there undiminished. On Christmas morning 1986 my mother dressed him, and my brother and I helped him to the car, and then we drove the short distance to my brother's house where everyone was waiting. We had our truly wonderful Christmas dinner, which of course my father couldn't eat. He said his goodbyes to all of the grandchildren and in the late afternoon we took him home.

My mum and I undressed him and put him to bed. Mum sat with him for about 15 minutes whilst I went for a walk and then, when I came home, I walked into his bedroom, held his hand and sat with him for a while. He told me that he was tired and that he had a full and wonderful life but that there had never been a day when he'd not thought about his fallen comrades and the randomness of why them and not him. He said he didn't fear what lay ahead and it was time to die. I was 26 years old and a junior officer in the RAF Regiment and whilst I was strong, and I completely understood, as I left his room that night I thought my heart would break.

About five in the morning my mum shouted for me and I went into their bedroom and she told me that she couldn't wake him. I checked for a pulse and checked his breathing; it was obvious he was still alive but he had slipped into a coma. I dialled for an ambulance and he was taken to hospital where 48 hours later he died quietly in his sleep and I was by his side.

I don't know why it's taken 25 years to write this book. Maybe it was time to record the story of an ordinary man who was so modest that he had never spoken of what he had done, not even to his family. Maybe it's also because after a full military career myself, I wanted my children and their children to know what their grandfather and his fellow warriors had achieved, and to share with the world a snapshot of an SAS soldier's life in World War 2.

In my military career I have been lucky enough to command some of the finest troops in the armed forces and have also been lucky to receive honours and awards, but there is an officers' saying (stolen from Sir Isaac Newton) which is that "we stand on the shoulders of giants". My dad never saw me collect either my Queen's Commendation or my MBE but he would have been proud and, in some small way, I knew he was with me in spirit when I did.

He was never decorated but the officers and men of 12 Commando, the Small Scale Raiding Force and 2nd SAS, with whom my father served his war, and with whom he risked his life, received amongst them many Distinguished Service Orders, Mentions in Dispatches and Military Medals. He never sought glory and was happy in quiet anonymity but Geoffrey Appleyard, PHP and every man he served with knew it wasn't about the man – it was always about the mission and the team. Through this book, I wanted to tell his story, the story of an unsung hero who lived no ordinary life.

Lightning Source UK Ltd.
Milton Keynes UK
UKOW03f2030201113

221519UK00002B/16/P